D1276883

# Mediterranean Cooking

**A STEP-BY-STEP GUIDE TO FABULOUS REGIONAL RECIPES AND TRADITIONS**

© Flame Tree Publishing 2009
Flame Tree is part of The Foundry Creative Media Company Limited

This 2009 edition published by Metro Books, by arrangement with The Foundry Creative Media Company Limited

All rights reserved. No part of this publication may be reproduced, stored in a retrieval system, or transmitted in any form or by any means, electronic, mechanical, photocopying, recording or otherwise, without the prior permission in writing of the publisher.

**Publisher and Creative Director:** Nick Wells
**Project Editor:** Catherine Taylor
**Picture Research:** Polly Prior
**Art Director & Layout Design:** Mike Spender
**Digital Design and Production:** Chris Herbert
**Proofreader:** Dawn Laker
**Indexer:** Helen Snaith

**Special thanks to:** Chelsea Edwards, Mark Ahrens and Katie Pimlott

All recipe photographs courtesy of Foundry Arts.

Non-recipe photographs courtesy of Shutterstock and copyright © the following photographers: 1 Courtney Keating; 3 & 148–49 Faraways;
4l & 23 Volfoni; 4r & 71t, 72r Paul Cowan; 5l & 128 Morozova Oksana; 6 & 84t Nolte Lourens; 68–69 Andrey Grinyov; 7 & 211 Catherine Jones; 10–11 Anobis;
8l & 158–59, 5r & 181r Phillip Lange; 8r & 135b Ramzi Hachicho; 9 & 76 Josef Bosak; 12 Istvan Csak; 13l Melisa Mok Mun Chee; 13r Jean Morrison; 14 Mandy Godbehear;
15l, 178r Vladimir Melnik; 15r, 181l Dhoxax; 16b Marek Slusarczyk; 16t Geanina Bechea; 17 Matt Trommer; 18–19 Heiko Meier; 20 bouzou; 21r archana bhartia;
22b Victoria Goncharenko; 22t Steve Beer; 24bl ivy photo; 24tl cyrrpit; 25 Filip Fuxa; 26–27 Elena Elisseeva; 28 ultimathule; 29l Patrycja Zadros; 29r inacio pires;
30 francesco riccardo iacomino; 31b Valeria73; 31t MARTAFR; 32b Dino; 32t Jeremy Reddington; 33 Yanta; 50–51 tomy; 70 Alan Kraft; 71b, 177b PixAchi; 72l Jan Martin Will;
73, 77l Sergey Kelin; 74–75 Christian Musat; 77r Tania Zbrodko; 78l BlueOrange Studio; 78r Emily Goodwin; 79 vospalej; 80 kucedra; 81b Netfalls; 81t Andrea Seemann;
82–83 Tomo Jesenicnik; 84b EVRON; 85r Mr. Kyryl Rudenko; 96–97 Agata Dorobek; 112–13 Ray Hub; 126–27 Rostislav Glinsky; 129l asliuzunoglu; 129r Maria Bell;
130, 170, 171b Holger Mette; 131l, 135t Styve Reineck; 131r RCH; 132–33 Sergey Petrov; 134l diak; 136 Evgeni Gitlits; 137b Arkady Mazor; 137t Pallando;
168–69 Gueorgui Ianakiev; 171t Amy Nichole Harris; 172b Clara; 172t Christophe Robard; 173, 178l WitR; 174–75 JIS; 176l Kit Oates;
177t Stana; 179 Anthony Maragou; 180 Boris Stroujko; 192–93 Mircea BEZERGHEANU

Metro Books
122 Fifth Avenue
New York, NY 10011

ISBN: 978-1-4351-1448-7

Printed and bound in China

1 3 5 7 9 10 8 6 4 2

# Mediterranean Cooking

## A STEP-BY-STEP GUIDE TO FABULOUS REGIONAL RECIPES AND TRADITIONS

**Diane & Jon Sutherland**

METRO BOOKS
NEW YORK

# Contents

# Introduction

**The sparkling, crystal-clear waters of the Mediterranean Sea connect a number of countries that may not always spring to mind as being 'Mediterranean'. But each of the countries covered in this book has a Mediterranean coastline and often a climate to match, so that their cuisine embodies many of the classic elements of Mediterranean cooking. In this exciting book we travel around the Mediterranean, from Spain, France and Italy in the west through to North Africa and Asia, via Greece, Crete and Cyprus in the east. We will discover the common characteristics and the traditions of food in the different countries. But we will also become aware that each of the countries has been influenced over the years by other Mediterranean countries, in addition to the climate and the choice of livestock and vegetables.**

## Health Benefits

People often refer to the 'Mediterranean diet', claiming that it is one of the healthiest diets in the world. However there is no one Mediterranean diet, as there are enormous differences in culture, ethnic background, religion, agricultural production and taste. Common threads that we will see in most of these Mediterranean diets and dishes is the relative high consumption of fruit, vegetables, potatoes, cereals, beans, nuts and seeds, as well as salads. With some notable exceptions dairy products are a lot less important than fish and poultry and, comparatively to

Europe or North America for example, very little red meat is eaten. Eggs are not consumed in the quantities seen in many other countries and, for many of these societies bordering the Mediterranean, where the grape is grown to create wine, the consumption levels of alcohol are surprisingly low.

More than half of the fat calories in a Mediterranean diet come from monounsaturated fats, which do not raise blood cholesterol levels in the same way that saturated fat does. This is one of the key reasons why the Mediterranean diet is considered to be so healthy. Olive oil, beloved of most Mediterranean cooking, is a vital source of monounsaturated fat. This means that the occurrence of heart disease in

Mediterranean countries is lower than in the rest of Europe or North America. Coupled with this is the lifestyle, with the tendency towards more physical activity and extended families. The commonly grown olive is claimed to have remarkable properties; not only does it provide monounsaturated fat, but it is also beneficial to the digestive system. Many claim that it not only helps to eliminate stomach ulcers but can also deal with internal infections and problems with the gall bladder. With so many major olive oil-producing countries around the Mediterranean Sea there is always stiff competition and lively debate as to which country produces the finest olive oil. In the west there are the vast olive groves of Spain and southern France, at the heart of the Mediterranean the Italian crop is grown and to the east each and every Greek island and parts of the mainland, together with vast, ancient plantations in Asia Minor, provide large quantities of the precious oil.

Following a strict Mediterranean diet has even been shown to provide protection against heart disease, cancer, Parkinson's disease and Alzheimer's. Effectively it is a lighter way of eating.

Much of the meat is grilled rather than fried or it is slow cooked in an oven. Desserts often include home grown fruits and honey is used to sweeten dishes rather than refined sugar.

## Culture

Food is an integral part of family life and culture across the whole of the Mediterranean. It is at the heart of people's hospitality. The flavours are robust, clear and uncomplicated and make full use of the gentle climate and the fertile soil. Onions, garlic, tomatoes and olive oil are at the heart of many of the dishes. Whilst Egyptians may prefer fava beans, the French favour green beans and the Tuscans cannellini beans. Yet these form the basis of very similar dishes. Proximity to the sea means that fish and shellfish feature in soups, stews and pastas. Smaller animals, such as sheep, goats and rabbit provide the majority of the meat. It is from sheep and goats that a great deal of the cheeses and yogurts are made.

Many people still cook in the traditional way, or using modern variations of open flames and simple ovens. Across the regions there are squashes, peppers, cucumbers, artichokes, okra, lettuces and a profusion of fresh herbs from rosemary and basil to fennel, mint and oregano.

# Identity

The various Mediterranean countries share far more than one virtually landlocked sea and an enormous beach around that ocean. They share a common heritage, a common perspective on life and food. They place their vegetables, fruits and livestock at the heart of their lives and their diets. For generations they have relied on the sea and the soil to provide them with timely, seasonal bounties of nutritious, largely organic and delicious food and drinks. Many of the traditional recipes have been passed down from generation to generation, mother to daughter, over the centuries. Yet from family to family, village to village and country to country these basic recipes have taken on separate identities, reflecting the culture and traditions of the people and the regions. No two Italian cooks, French chefs or Greek taverna owners will agree with even the essential

ingredients of a common sauce or simple vegetable dish. The dishes have evolved with experimentation and the use of regional or seasonal variations.

Mediterranean food is a feast for meat lovers, seafood devotees and for vegetarians. There is something in the diet for everyone and for any occasion. For Mediterranean people food is something to be shared and lingered over. They are fiercely proud of their culinary heritage, whether it has a distinctly French, Greek, Italian, Spanish or Moroccan influence. *Mediterranean Cooking* gives you a taste of the dishes that are served in luxurious villas on the French Riviera, in the hills of Tuscany, on the mosaic of Greek islands or in exotic Marrakesh. The recipes incorporate the basics of style and technique, but also show you the more sophisticated Mediterranean recipes; it is a cookbook that entertains as well as educates.

# Western Europe

From pizza and pasta to paella and tapas,
from French fine dining to hearty moussaka,
Western Europe's Mediterranean countries
have a diverse culinary tradition.

Spain

Surrounded by water and situated at the crossroads of the Mediterranean Sea and the Atlantic Ocean, Spain has an ancient maritime tradition, which is reflected in its cuisine. Influenced by fresh seafood and healthy, home-grown produce, the country's history, culture and different regions all contribute to its varied array of dishes. It has a predominantly dry and mountainous terrain, although its varied landscape ranges from lush countryside to rugged coastlines. The mountainous areas are perfect terrain for the rearing of goats and sheep, both of which are used in many Spanish recipes.

The tradition of growing wheat flourished during Roman times. Its quality was so good that the trend for using the grain had already spread throughout Spain, Greece and parts of North Africa. Onions and garlic were introduced to the Spaniards by the Phoenicians and tomatoes, potatoes and peppers from South America or the Caribbean. The Romans heavily influenced Spanish cuisine, as did the Moors, who left behind the use of honey and cumin in Spanish dishes, particularly those dishes that are still cooked in the southern regions of the country today. The Moors also introduced the use of almonds and egg yolks in the making of Spanish desserts.

There are several recipes that are common to the various regions of Spain, including Tortilla de Patata (potato omelette), paella, stews, such as Pork Stew with Saffron Rice, and recipes

based on pulses, such as chickpeas and lentils, as the major ingredient. But the regional variations in recipes make Spain's cuisine even more diverse. Madrid is famous for Cocido Madrileño (chickpea stew) and Callos a la Madrilène (made from tripe). Catalonia has a long tradition of being famous for its rice dishes and the quality of its seafood. Despite this, perhaps the best-known Catalonian dish is Crema Catalana, very much like a crème brûlée. Other favourite Spanish desserts include flans, and cakes such as Madeleines, as well as custard, rice pudding, torrijas and churros. Torrijas are slices of bread soaked in milk and sugar (or sometimes wine), coated in egg, fried in oil and drizzled with syrup or honey, or sprinkled with sugar and cinnamon. Churros are similar to doughnuts and named for their shape, which is said to resemble the horns of the sheep bred in Castile. Churros can be thick or thin and are usually dipped in coffee or hot chocolate at breakfast time.

The region of La Rioja, as well producing its well-known wine, is renowned for its vegetable soups and its pepper and potato dishes, while in the west of Spain the area of Extremadura is famous for Cocido Extremeño, a rich stew made from bacon, poultry, ham and vegetables. Andalucia has a long tradition of fish and seafood, especially shrimps, squid, mackerel and flat fish, and Murcia is known for fish and lamb stews. Valencia, the home of Spain's famous paella, still celebrates public holidays by cooking huge dishes of paella in the streets, making them as colourful and tempting as possible. Paella is popular throughout Spain, including the islands, and traditionally families enjoy the dish at Sunday lunchtime.

The central region of Spain is unsurprisingly less influenced by the sea and is well known for roast meats, such as lamb, veal, and young pigs and goats. The meat is roasted slowly in a wood-fired oven until it is extremely tender and full of flavour.

The Balearic Islands of Mallorca, Menorca, Ibiza and Formentera have a typical Catalonian tradition of seafood dishes, together with simple dishes predominantly comprising vegetables. Tumbet, a dish of fried potatoes, peppers and aubergine in a tomato stew similar to France's

ratatouille is a prime example, although Majorca in particular is renowned for its pastries, called Ensaimadas, which are warm, yeast-based cakes that are made into round, coiled shapes. They are sliced into individual portions and served with hot coffee or drinking chocolate, much like Churros.

The famous Spanish tradition of a tapas bar can be found in even the smallest of Spanish villages. The word *tapa* means 'lid' (from *tapar*, 'to cover'), so the use of this word to mean 'snack' is believed to have originated from the plate of appetizers that hosts would place over their guests' glasses to prevent flies entering the glasses. There is no absolute recipe for tapas; they can include cheeses, fish, eggs, vegetables, dips and pastries or can simply be a slice of toasted bread dipped in olive oil and garlic, a dish of olives, slices of ham or salami, pieces of Spanish tortilla or marinated anchovies. Meatballs in tomato sauce, garlic mushrooms, shrimp or cooked chorizo in wine are all offered in tapas bars around Spain. Tapas are displayed on or in the bar for guests to choose.

Certainly olive oil is an indispensable ingredient of many Spanish recipes, as is garlic, which is added to most dishes. Spanish cooking uses a variety of meat in large quantities, depending on farming and tradition in the region. Chicken, pork and rabbit feature frequently, as do sausages and salamis, particularly chorizo, which is a spicy and very popular Spanish sausage. Also popular are prawns, shrimps, anchovies and sardines.

Gazpacho is a famous Spanish soup, made from a mixture of tomato, olive oil, garlic, cucumbers and croutons, and is served chilled. As for drinks, sangria is a red wine and fruit punch that can be found everywhere in Spain and Rioja (from La Rioja in northern Spain) is one of Spain's leading varieties of wine, together with Valdepeñas and a number of Cavas, which are sparkling wines. Jerez, or Spanish sherry, is regularly consumed in Spanish bars, restaurants and homes.

**France**

**France's reputation for *haute cuisine* has evolved over the centuries, but there still remains a diverse regional recipe variation. The French have a refined style of cooking, which is the result of both political and social changes throughout the centuries. Some of their national dishes and recipes originated as regional ones, particularly their breads and cheeses, but the fall of the monarchy during the French Revolution put many chefs out of work and they were forced to sell food to the general public through their newly established restaurants, rather than cook for the rich and famous.**

Until this time the diet of the French peasant had consisted mainly of what they could grow themselves. But by 1914 and the First World War, with improved distribution and transportation throughout France, different foods and cattle were introduced to the recipes of the general public. Three main chefs are credited with refining French cuisine over the centuries, namely François Pierre de la Varenne (1618–78), Marie-Antoine Carême (1784–1833) and Georges Auguste Escoffier (1846–1935), the latter being possibly the most influential of the three. Escoffier introduced lighter sauces and reduced the number of spices used in the recipes, as well as laying down set procedures for subsequent cooks to follow.

When referring to Mediterranean cuisine and France, you can only really mean the southern half of France, more particularly the coastal regions. Southern France is colloquially known as Le

Midi ('noon' in French, derived from the old French for 'middle' and 'day'), as the sun is always in the south at noon in France (and the rest of the Northern Hemisphere). One significant part of southern France is the Languedoc-Roussillon region (pictured page 24, left), which is particularly famed for its vineyards around Bordeaux, although it also produces abundant cheeses, olive oils and pies known as Petits Pâtés de Pezenas. But the really Mediterranean feel starts when you reach Provence, the Riviera and the French island of Corsica…

In these areas, olive trees are grown in abundance; the warmer climate and proximity of these regions to the Mediterranean Sea make the production of olive oil a successful industry here. Provence olive oil is of the highest quality and enhances many traditional Provençal recipes, used instead of the butters and creams used in many other parts of France. Provence also boasts an abundance of fresh fruit and vegetables, which are complemented by the wide range of herbs, many of which can be found growing wild throughout the region. Honey is the natural sweetener for many Provence recipes, made by the bees from the Provençal wild flowers and the carpets of

lavender for which the region is famous. Fish from the Mediterranean Sea are simply grilled, as is the locally reared meat, which has thrived from eating the wild rosemary growing throughout the area.

Provençal specialities range from simple salads to stuffed vegetables, grilled lamb chops served with herbs de Provence and the famous fish dish bouillabaisse. This dish is made with at least three kinds of fresh fish cooked in a broth with onions, tomatoes, saffron and various herbs, such as laurel, sage and thyme. The soup is served with toast and rouille, a spicy sauce that some mix into the broth and others choose to spread onto the toast. The most renowned bouillabaisse dish is cooked

in the city of Marseille. Other Provençal dishes have been influenced by the region's geography; in the north the mountain cuisine is based on cheese and cured meats, whilst in the south the Mediterranean Sea provides its bounty of fish.

The cuisine of the sunny Côte d'Azur or French Riviera uses olive oil, citrus fruits and aromatic herbs in many dishes, but also incorporates produce from the inner regions of France, such as young kid, strong cheeses and fresh vegetables. This region's dishes tend to be a blend of French and Italian cuisine, using a mix of olive oil and butter, with the influences of several Mediterranean countries appearing in the dishes from time to time. Salade Niçoise is a speciality of the Côte D'Azur,

originating in and named after the city of Nice and made popular during the 1880s. Served on a flat plate, ripe tomato wedges, halved boiled new potatoes, steamed green beans and wedges of hard-boiled eggs are arranged on a bed of crisp lettuce and topped with tinned tuna in olive oil and Niçoise olives. The salad is garnished with tinned anchovies and served with traditional Dijon vinaigrette.

A world away from mainland France, goats and sheep inhabit the island of Corsica (Bonifacio pictured opposite and page 25) in abundance, so it is not surprising that the meat from kids and lambs are used in traditional Corsican dishes, such as the meat stew known as stufato, and ragout, also a meat stew that can be added to pasta dishes. The Corsicans also enjoy simple, roasted meat dishes. The island's home-reared pork is used to make hams, dried pork fillet, dried sausage, Pancetta, bacon and smoked and dried liverwurst. Chestnuts are grown in the Corsican Castagniccia forest and are used to produce

flour for making bread, cakes and polenta. Acorns from the Castagniccia forest are also used as animal food for the island's pigs and boars. Fresh fish and seafood dishes are served regularly, as are the locally grown clementines, lemons, nectarines and figs. Candied citrus fruit is used in cake recipes and to make nougat, and the island's brocciu cheese, made from sheep's or goats' milk, together with the chestnuts, are used in Corsica's dessert recipes.

Italy

The 'boot' of Italy, along with its islands of Sicily and Sardinia, sits proudly in the centre of the Mediterranean Sea and, with its roots dating back to before Christ, modern-day Italian cuisine is one of the most popular in the Mediterranean, and in fact the world.

There are distinctions between the recipes of the north and south of Italy, as well as between deep inland and the coastal regions and islands, mainly because of Italy's history of European cultures – from the Etruscans and the Romans to the Renaissance and the Baroque. It was the discovery of the New World that brought about the introduction of potatoes, tomatoes, bell peppers and maize to Italy and it was during the Middle Ages that food preservation, by smoking or bottling in brine, became an important role for any cook. Because the Mediterranean trade routes were strongly controlled by the Arab countries, the southern regions of Italy were heavily influenced by this in their choice of recipes. But the Roman and Germanic cultures strongly affected the northern regions. Certainly over the years the development of regional Italian recipes and cuisine has progressed. Each region has its own specialities, which has stemmed from bordering countries like France and Austria, or the closeness to the Mediterranean Sea or the mountains. Italian cuisine is seasonal and boasts the use of fresh, locally grown produce.

The recipes of Italy's northeastern region of Fruili-Venezia Giulia are influenced by Austria, Hungary, Slovenia and Croatia with sausages, goulash, sauerkraut, dumplings, strudels and polenta,

Piedmont's preferred preserved dish is Filetto Baciato, which involves a white-wine-marinated pork fillet being coated with salami paste and cured for at least six months.

The north-Italian region of Emilia-Romagna is reputedly the pasta capital, laying claim to many of its own pasta types and dishes, including Bologna's famed tagliatelle and meat sauce. However, polenta was in fact the former staple at least of many mountainous areas of this region, particularly in the Apennine Mountain towns and villages. There is also a tradition for producing balsamic vinegar, Parmesan cheese, Parma, pancetta and other cured hams.

used as an accompaniment to meat, fish and cheese dishes. With Venice as its capital city, the region of Veneto is famous for risotto, made from seafood on the coast, or from pumpkin, asparagus, radish or frogs' legs inland, as well as dishes of pasta and borlotti or cannellini beans, such as Pasta Fagioli. Risotto is also popular in Lombardy, as are rice soups and regional cheeses like Gorgonzola, but heartier soups and roasted and braised meats are customary in the Val D'Aosta region. Surrounded on three sides by the Alps and with Turin as its capital, the region of Piedmont relies on the changing seasons for its recipes. Fish, nuts, garlic, truffles, vegetables and fungi are all used regularly and the cheese Castelmagno is produced.

Tuscany and Umbria boast many simple, home-grown foods. Mushrooms, vegetables, fruit, olives, herbs, truffles and freshly caught fish are popular and in the coastal area of Marche, in addition to fish and seafood, sausages and home-cured ham are produced. Neighbouring Lazio's cuisine is heartier and shows signs of a Jewish influence in its use of artichokes and spicy and hearty pasta dishes, whilst to the east, the people of Abruzzo prefer hot and spicy lamb and pasta dishes, flavoured with their locally grown chillies. The Abruzzo area is renowned for its production of saffron, which is used in many Italian dishes.

In Campania (Prócida and Capri islands, in the Gulf of Naples, are pictured opposite and on page 33 respectively), durum wheat is used to make pasta, and sauces and pizzas are often topped with the region's mozzarella cheese, made from water buffalo milk. Dried durum wheat pasta is also an important export of the Apulia (Puglia) region, also in the south, where olive oil production is the highest in the country. The people of neighbouring Basilicata prefer to have meat as the accompaniment to their durum wheat pasta, particularly pork.

In the 'toe' of Italy, Calabria has a varied cultural past and this is reflected in its people's favourite recipes – the Arabs introduced citrus fruits, raisins, artichokes and aubergines, for instance, and cookery skills were influenced during the House of Anjou and Napoleon Bonaparte eras and by the Spanish. Much seafood and fresh fish is eaten in this region and melons and watermelons are grown as a local speciality.

The islands of Sicily and Sardinia (pictured above and on page 28 respectively) have their own speciality dishes. Sicilian cuisine was influenced by the Ancient Greeks (wine),

the Romans (goose) and the Byzantines, who introduced many new flavours to the island. During the tenth and eleventh centuries the Arabs introduced more new flavours, with apricots, sugar, citrus fruits, melons, rice, raisins and spices, such as nutmeg, clove and cinnamon. Later, in 1194, the Hohenstaufens became the Germanic Kings of Sicily and influenced the diet with the introduction of meats, and then the Spanish became the main influence by introducing cocoa, maize, tomatoes and turkey. Being islands, Sicilians and Sardinians enjoy seafood and fish, such as rock lobster, scampi, squid, tuna, sardines, cuttlefish and swordfish.

As with many Mediterranean countries, the Italians enjoy appetizers, such as antipasti washed down with a good wine. These snack-size portions are often also eaten between meals or to accompany drinks for guests, as it is considered impolite or unhealthy to serve alcohol without food. Like the varying specialities and cuisines throughout Italy, there is also a wide variety of wine-producing regions, totalling around 20 throughout the country, producing the largest amount of wine in the world and regulated very closely by the Italian government.

Mediterran

# Starters & Salads

With such a wonderful climate, it is little wonder that most of the Mediterranean countries can enjoy fresh produce throughout the year. Their salads, fruit and vegetables are virtually grown on their doorsteps, picked on the day of use and the flavours are out of this world.

Mediterranean appetizers are not always used at the beginning of a meal, but often as a snack or to accompany drinks – think 'tapas' and 'antipasti'. Most of the salads and starters covered in this section are quick and easy to prepare, they are irresistible, they taste amazing and the added bonus is that they are usually healthy too!

# Roasted Aubergine Dip with Pitta Strips

This dish is a variation on the traditional Arabic dish known as Baba Ganoush, which translates to 'spoilt old man', but similar dips are also common in Greece and Turkey.

Preheat the oven to 180C°/350°F/Gas Mark 4. On a chopping board, cut the pitta breads into strips. Spread the bread in a single layer on a large baking sheet. Cook in the preheated oven for 15 minutes until golden and crisp. Leave to cool on a wire cooling rack.

Trim the aubergines/eggplants, rinse lightly and reserve. Heat a griddle pan until almost smoking. Cook the aubergines and garlic for about 15 minutes. Turn the aubergines frequently, until very tender with wrinkled and charred skins. Remove from heat and leave to cool.

When the aubergines are cool enough to handle, cut in half and scoop out the cooked flesh and place in a food processor. Squeeze the softened garlic flesh from the papery skin and add to the aubergine. Blend the aubergine and garlic until smooth. Add the sesame oil, lemon juice and cumin and blend again to mix. Season to taste with salt and pepper, stir in the parsley.

Serve with the pitta strips and mixed salad leaves.

## INGREDIENTS        Serves 4

- **4 pitta breads**
- **2 large aubergines/eggplants**
- **1 garlic clove, peeled**
- **¼ tsp sesame oil**
- **1 tbsp lemon juice**
- **½ tsp ground cumin**
- **salt and freshly ground black pepper**
- **2 tbsp freshly chopped parsley**
- **fresh salad leaves, to serve**

## HELPFUL HINT

As well as being great with pitta strips or bread sticks, this dish is fantastic warmed through and served as a meal accompaniment.

# Aubergine & Yogurt Dip

Roasting the aubergines gives this dish a much more mellow flavour. Serve it alone, or as part of a tempting array of dips with naan or pitta.

Preheat the oven to 200°C/400°F/Gas Mark 6. Pierce the skin of the aubergines/eggplants with a fork and place on a baking tray. Cook for 40 minutes or until very soft.

Cool the aubergines, then cut in half, scoop out the flesh and tip into a bowl.

Mash the aubergine with the olive oil, lemon juice and garlic until smooth or blend for a few seconds in a food processor.

Chop the pimientos into small dice and add to the aubergine mixture.

When blended, add the yogurt. Stir well and season to taste with salt and pepper.

Add the chopped olives and leave in the refrigerator to chill for at least 30 minutes.

Place the cauliflower and broccoli florets and carrot strips into a frying pan and cover with boiling water. Simmer for 2 minutes, then rinse in cold water. Drain and serve as crudités to accompany the dip.

## INGREDIENTS
**Makes 600 ml/1 pint/2½ cups**

- **2 x 225 g/½ lb aubergines/eggplants**
- **1 tbsp light olive oil**
- **1 tbsp lemon juice**
- **2 garlic cloves, peeled and crushed**
- **190 g/6.5 oz jar pimientos, drained**
- **150 ml/¼ pint/⅔ cup low-fat natural yogurt**
- **salt and freshly ground black pepper**
- **25 g/1 oz/¼ cup black olives, pitted and chopped**
- **225 g/8 oz/2¼ cups cauliflower florets**
- **225 g/8 oz/2¼ cups broccoli florets**
- **125 g/4 oz/1 cup carrots, peeled and cut into 5 cm/2 inch strips**

## TASTY TIP

If serving with naan or pitta, try warming the bread first. Preheat the oven to 200°C/400°F/Gas Mark 6, wrap in preheated kitchen foil and place in the oven for 5–7 minutes depending on the size of the bread.

# Mushroom & Red Wine Pâté

This pâté is almost a meal in itself and full of interesting flavours, all of which seem to burst into life in the mouth.

Preheat the oven to 180°C/350°F/Gas Mark 4. Cut the bread in half diagonally. Place the bread triangles on a baking tray and cook for 10 minutes.

Remove from the oven and split each bread triangle in half to make 12 triangles, then return to the oven until golden and crisp. Leave to cool on a wire rack.

Heat the oil in a saucepan and gently cook the onion and garlic until transparent.

Add the mushrooms and cook, stirring, for 3–4 minutes, or until the mushroom juices start to run.

Stir the wine and herbs into the mushroom mixture and bring to the boil. Reduce the heat and simmer uncovered until all the liquid is absorbed. Remove from the heat and season to taste with salt and pepper. Leave to cool.

When cold, beat in the soft cream cheese and adjust the seasoning. Place in a small clean bowl and chill until required. Serve the toast triangles with the cucumber and tomato.

## INGREDIENTS          Serves 4

- **3 large slices white bread, crusts removed**
- **2 tsp olive oil**
- **1 small onion, peeled and finely chopped**
- **1 garlic clove, peeled and crushed**
- **350 g/12 oz/5 cups button/white mushrooms, wiped and finely chopped**
- **150 ml/¼ pint/⅔ cup red wine**
- **½ tsp dried mixed herbs**
- **1 tbsp freshly chopped parsley**
- **salt and freshly ground black pepper**
- **2 tbsp low-fat cream cheese**

### To serve:
- **finely chopped cucumber**
- **finely chopped tomato**

# Wild Rice Dolmades

This vegetarian version of Greek stuffed vine leaves is also eaten in Turkey and Middle Eastern countries. Minced lamb can be added for meat eaters.

Heat 1 tbsp of the oil in a frying pan and gently cook the pine nuts for 2–3 minutes, stirring frequently, until golden. Remove from the pan and reserve.

Add 1½ tablespoons oil to the pan and gently cook the mushrooms, spring onions/scallions and garlic for 7–8 minutes until very soft. Stir in the rice, herbs, salt and pepper.

Put a heaped teaspoon of stuffing in the centre of each leaf (if the leaves are small, put two together, overlapping slightly). Fold over the stalk end, then the sides, and roll up to make a neat parcel. Continue until all the stuffing is used.

Arrange the stuffed leaves close together, seam-side down, in a large saucepan, drizzling each with a little of the remaining oil. There will be several layers. Pour over enough stock to cover.

Put an inverted plate over the dolmades to stop them unrolling during cooking. Bring to the boil, then simmer very gently for 3 minutes. Cool in the saucepan.

Transfer the dolmades to a serving dish. Cover and chill in the refrigerator before serving. Sprinkle with the pine nuts and garnish with lemon and dill. Serve.

## INGREDIENTS    Serves 4-6

- **6 tbsp olive oil**
- **2½ tbsp pine nuts**
- **175 g/6 oz/1¾ cups mushrooms, wiped and finely chopped**
- **4 spring onions/scallions, trimmed and finely chopped**
- **1 garlic clove, peeled and crushed**
- **50 g/2 oz/⅓ cup cooked wild rice**
- **2 tsp freshly chopped dill**
- **2 tsp freshly chopped mint**
- **salt and freshly ground black pepper**
- **16–24 prepared medium vine/grape leaves**
- **about 300 ml/½ pint/1¼ cups vegetable stock**

**To garnish:**
- **lemon wedges**
- **fresh dill sprigs**

## HELPFUL HINT

Fresh vine leaves are available in early summer and should be blanched for 2–3 minutes in boiling water. Vine leaves preserved in brine can be found all year round in supermarkets – soak in warm water for 20 minutes before using.

# Olive & Feta Parcels

No need to add seasoning to this richly flavoured dish as olives and feta are quite salty; bet your guests cannot resist eating more than one!

Preheat the oven to 180°C/350°F/Gas Mark 4. Preheat the grill/broiler, then line the rack with kitchen foil.

Cut the peppers into quarters and remove the seeds. Place skin-side up on the foil-lined rack and cook under the preheated grill for 10 minutes, turning occasionally until the skins begin to blacken. Place the peppers in a polythene/plastic bag and leave until cool enough to handle, then skin and thinly slice.

Chop the olives and cut the feta cheese into small cubes. Mix together the olives, feta, sliced peppers and pine nuts.

Cut a sheet of pastry dough in half, then brush with a little of the oil. Place a spoonful of the olive and feta mix about one-third of the way up the dough. Fold over the dough and wrap to form a square package encasing the filling completely.

Place this package in the centre of the second half of the dough sheet.

Brush the edges lightly with a little oil, bring up the corners to meet in the centre and twist them loosely to form a pocket. Brush with a little more oil and repeat with the remaining dough and filling.

Place the pockets on a lightly oiled baking sheet and bake in the preheated oven for 10–15 minutes, or until crisp and golden brown. Serve with the dip.

## INGREDIENTS          Makes 30

- **1 small red and 1 small yellow pepper**
- **125 g/4½ oz/⅔ cup assorted marinated green and black olives**
- **125 g/4½ oz feta cheese**
- **2 tbsp pine nuts, lightly toasted**
- **6 sheets filo/phyllo pastry dough**
- **3 tbsp olive oil**
- **sour cream and chive dip, to serve**

## HELPFUL HINT

Feta is generally made from goats' milk and has quite a salty taste. To make the cheese less salty simply soak it in milk, then drain before eating.

# French Onion Tart

The French are known for baking tarts and this recipe is typical of the art. A more Provençale version involves anchovies, capers and olives.

Preheat the oven to 200°C/400°F/Gas Mark 6. Place the butter in the freezer for 30 minutes. Sift the flour and salt into a large bowl. Remove the butter from the freezer and grate using the coarse side of a grater, dipping the butter in the flour every now and again to make it easier to grate.

Mix the butter into the flour, using a palette knife, making sure all the butter is thoroughly coated with flour. Add 2 tablespoons cold water and continue to mix, bringing the mixture together. Use your hands to complete the mixing. Add a little more water if needed to leave a clean bowl. Place the pastry dough in a polythene/plastic bag and chill in the refrigerator for 30 minutes.

Heat the oil in a large frying pan, then fry the onions for 10 minutes, stirring occasionally, until softened. Stir in the white wine vinegar and muscovado/dark brown sugar. Increase the heat and stir frequently for another 4–5 minutes until the onions turn a deep caramel colour. Cook for another 5 minutes, then reserve to cool.

On a lightly floured surface, roll out the pastry dough to a 35 cm/14 inch round. Wrap over a rolling pin and lift the round onto a baking sheet.

Sprinkle half the cheese over the dough, leaving a 5 cm/2 inch border around the edge, then spoon the caramelized onions over the cheese.

Fold the uncovered dough edges over the edge of the filling to form a rim. Brush the rim with beaten egg or milk.

Season to taste with salt and pepper. Sprinkle over the remaining cheese and bake for 20–25 minutes. Transfer to a large plate and serve immediately.

## INGREDIENTS          Serves 4

### For the quick flaky pastry:
- 125 g/4½ oz/1 stick plus 1 tbsp butter
- 175 g/6 oz/1½ cups plain/all-purpose flour
- a pinch salt

### For the filling:
- 2 tbsp olive oil
- 4 large onions, peeled and thinly sliced
- 3 tbsp white wine vinegar
- 2 tbsp muscovado/dark brown sugar
- 175 g/6 oz/1½ cups grated Cheddar cheese
- some beaten egg or milk
- salt and freshly ground black pepper

## TASTY TIP

For a milder, nutty taste, substitute the Cheddar cheese for Gruyère and grate a little nutmeg over the second layer of cheese.

# Garlic Wild Mushrooms Galettes

Galettes are traditional French savoury or sweet tarts using rich flaky pastry. The word is also used in France to refer to savoury buckwheat crepes.

Preheat the oven to 220°C/425°F/Gas Mark 7. On a lightly floured surface, roll out the chilled pastry dough very thinly. Cut out 6 x 15 cm/6 inch circles and place on a lightly oiled baking sheet.

Divide the onion into rings and reserve. Wipe or lightly rinse the mushrooms. Half or quarter any large mushrooms and keep the small ones whole. Heat the butter in a frying pan and fry the onion, chilli and garlic gently for about 3 minutes. Add the mushrooms and cook for about 5 minutes, or until beginning to soften.

Stir the parsley into the mushroom mixture and drain off any excess liquid. Pile the mushroom mixture onto the pastry circles within 5 mm/¼ inch of the edges. Arrange the sliced mozzarella cheese on top. Bake in the preheated oven for 12–15 minutes, or until golden brown, and serve with the tomatoes and salad.

## INGREDIENTS · Serves 6

- **1 quantity quick flaky pastry dough (see French Onion Tart, page 46), chilled**
- **1 onion, peeled and thinly sliced**
- **275 g/10 oz/2½ cups mixed mushrooms, e.g. oyster, chestnut/crimini, morels, chanterelles**
- **25 g/1 oz/¼ stick butter**
- **1 red chilli, deseeded and thinly sliced**
- **2 garlic cloves, peeled and very thinly sliced**
- **2 tbsp freshly chopped parsley**
- **125 g/4½ oz mozzarella cheese, sliced**

**To serve:**
- **cherry tomatoes**
- **mixed green salad leaves**

## HELPFUL HINT

Many supermarkets now stock a variety of wild mushrooms, all of which can be used in this recipe. It is important to maintain as much of the flavour of the mushrooms as possible, so do not peel mushrooms unless they appear old or tough. Either rinse lightly if covered with small pieces of soil or wipe well, trim the stalks and use.

# Mediterranean Potato Salad

With such an array of fresh produce, it is unsurprising that this is a popular dish in most Mediterranean countries and packed with vitamins too.

Preheat the oven to 200°C/400°F/Gas Mark 6. Place the potatoes in a large saucepan of salted water, bring to the boil and simmer until just tender. Do not overcook. Drain and plunge into cold water, to stop them from cooking further.

Place the onions in a bowl with the peppers. Pour over 2 tablespoons of the olive oil. Stir and spoon onto a large baking tray. Cook in the preheated oven for 25–30 minutes, or until the vegetables are tender and lightly charred in places, stirring occasionally. Remove from the oven and transfer to a large bowl.

Cut the potatoes into bite-sized pieces and mix with the roasted onions and peppers. Add the tomatoes and olives to the potatoes. Crumble over the feta cheese and sprinkle with the chopped parsley.

Whisk together the remaining olive oil, vinegar, mustard and honey, then season to taste with salt and pepper. Pour the dressing over the potatoes and toss gently together. Garnish with parsley sprigs and serve immediately.

## INGREDIENTS  Serves 4

- **700 g/1½ lb/about 6 small waxy potatoes**
- **2 red onions, peeled and roughly chopped**
- **1 yellow pepper, deseeded and roughly chopped**
- **1 green pepper, deseeded and roughly chopped**
- **6 tbsp extra virgin olive oil**
- **125 g/4½ oz/⅓ cup ripe tomatoes, chopped**
- **50 g/2 oz/½ cup pitted black olives, sliced**
- **125 g/4½ oz feta cheese**
- **3 tbsp freshly chopped parsley**
- **2 tbsp white wine vinegar**
- **1 tsp Dijon mustard**
- **1 tsp clear honey**
- **salt and freshly ground black pepper**
- **sprigs fresh parsley, to garnish**

## FOOD FACT

Tomatoes are such an integral part of many cuisines, that it is hard to believe they were only introduced to Europe from the Americas a few hundred years ago. There are lots of new flavoursome varieties now available to try. Those sold still attached to the vine tend to have a particularly good flavour.

# Italian Bean Soup

This hearty soup encompasses everything Italian, from tomatoes on the vine to pasta, oregano, garlic, fresh herbs and olive oil; and it will taste even better the day after it has been made.

Heat the oil in a large saucepan. Add the leek, garlic and oregano and cook gently for 5 minutes, stirring occasionally.

Stir in the French/green beans and the cannellini beans. Sprinkle in the pasta and pour in the stock.

Bring the stock mixture to the boil, then reduce the heat to a simmer.

Cook for 12–15 minutes, or until the vegetables are tender and the pasta is cooked to *al dente*. Stir occasionally.

In a heavy-based frying pan, dry-fry the tomatoes over a high heat until they soften and the skins begin to blacken.

Gently crush the tomatoes in the pan with the back of a spoon and add to the soup.

Season to taste with salt and pepper. Stir in the shredded basil and serve immediately.

## INGREDIENTS          Serves 4

- **2 tsp olive oil**
- **1 leek, washed and chopped**
- **1 garlic clove, peeled and crushed**
- **2 tsp dried oregano**
- **75 g/3 oz/¾ cup French/green beans, trimmed and cut into bite-sized pieces**
- **410 g/14 oz can cannellini beans, drained and rinsed**
- **75 g/3 oz/½ cup small pasta shapes**
- **1 litre/1¾ pint/1 quart vegetable stock**
- **8 cherry tomatoes**
- **salt and freshly ground black pepper**
- **3 tbsp freshly shredded basil**

## FOOD FACT

The majority of Italian cooking takes advantage of the abundance of freshly grown herbs, especially when used in tomato-based dishes. With a few exceptions, where possible it is worth trying to use fresh herbs to draw out the other flavours of the dish. However, if you decide to use dried herbs remember that they are much more pungent. 1 teaspoon of dried herbs equals roughly 1 tablespoon of fresh herbs.

# Roasted Red Pepper, Tomato & Red Onion Soup

Full of flavour and a rich, tempting colour, this Mediterranean soup is packed full of goodness and could be kept safely in the fridge overnight.

Preheat the oven to 190°C/375°F/Gas Mark 5. Spray a large roasting tin/pan with the oil and place the peppers and onion in the base. Cook in the oven for 10 minutes. Add the tomatoes and cook for a further 20 minutes, or until the peppers are soft.

Cut the bread into 1 cm/½ inch slices. Cut the garlic clove in half and rub the cut edge over the bread.

Place all the bread slices on a large baking sheet and bake in the preheated oven for 10 minutes, turning halfway through, until golden and crisp.

Remove the vegetables from the oven and allow to cool slightly, then blend in a food processor until smooth. Strain the vegetable mixture through a large nylon sieve/strainer into a saucepan, to remove the seeds and skin. Add the stock, season to taste with salt and pepper and stir to mix. Heat the soup gently until piping hot.

In a small bowl, beat together the Worcestershire sauce with the fromage frais/reduced-fat sour cream. Pour the soup into warmed bowls and swirl a spoonful of the fromage frais mixture into each bowl. Serve immediately with the garlic toast.

### INGREDIENTS          Serves 4

- **fine spray of olive oil**
- **2 large red peppers, deseeded and roughly chopped**
- **1 red onion, peeled and roughly chopped**
- **3 tomatoes, halved**
- **1 small crusty French loaf**
- **1 garlic clove, peeled**
- **600 ml/1 pint/2½ cups vegetable stock**
- **salt and freshly ground black pepper**
- **1 tsp Worcestershire sauce**
- **4 tbsp fromage frais/reduced-fat sour cream**

### HELPFUL HINT

A quick, hassle-free way to remove the skin from peppers once they have been roasted or grilled is to place them in a polythene/plastic bag. Leave for 10 minutes, or until cool enough to handle, then simply peel the skin away from the flesh.

# Mediterranean Chowder

With the Mediterranean Sea on their doorsteps, little wonder that this is a popular, healthy and wholesome fish-based soup or stew in many Mediterranean countries.

Heat the oil and butter together in a large saucepan, add the onion, celery and garlic and cook gently for 2–3 minutes until softened. Add the chilli and stir in the flour. Cook, stirring, for a further minute.

Add the potatoes to the saucepan with the stock. Bring to the boil, cover and simmer for 10 minutes. Add the fish cubes to the saucepan with the chopped parsley and cook for a further 5–10 minutes, or until the fish and potatoes are just tender.

Stir in the peeled prawns/shrimp and sweetcorn and season to taste with salt and pepper. Pour in the cream and adjust the seasoning, if necessary.

Scatter the snipped chives over the top of the chowder. Ladle into 6 large bowls and serve immediately with plenty of warm crusty bread.

## FOOD FACT

A chowder is a classic meal-in-a-bowl soup whose name originates from the French chaudière (the pot used by settlers in the southern states of America for making soups and stews). Chowders are usually fish based and often feature sweetcorn. This version has been thickened with potatoes.

## INGREDIENTS　　　Serves 6

- **1 tbsp olive oil**
- **1 tbsp butter**
- **1 large onion, peeled and finely sliced**
- **4 celery stalks, trimmed and thinly sliced**
- **2 garlic cloves, peeled and crushed**
- **1 bird's-eye chilli, deseeded and finely chopped**
- **1 tbsp plain/all-purpose flour**
- **225 g/8 oz/1¼ cups potatoes, peeled and diced**
- **600 ml/1 pint/2½ cups fish or vegetable stock**
- **700 g/1½ lb whiting or cod fillet cut into 2.5 cm/1 inch cubes**
- **2 tbsp freshly chopped parsley**
- **125 g/4 oz/1½ cups large peeled prawns/shrimp**
- **198 g/7 oz can sweetcorn, drained**
- **salt and freshly ground black pepper**
- **150 ml/¼ pint/⅔ cup single/light cream**
- **1 tbsp freshly snipped chives**
- **warm, crusty bread, to serve**

# Mediterranean Feast

This healthy Niçoise salad-like dish combines many of the ingredients that are cultivated in most Mediterranean countries, often in the back gardens of the local people.

Cut the lettuce into four and remove the hard core. Tear into bite-sized pieces and arrange on a large serving platter or four individual plates.

Cook the French/green beans in boiling salted water for 8 minutes and the potatoes for 10 minutes, or until tender. Drain and rinse in cold water until cool, then cut both the beans and potatoes in half with a sharp knife.

Boil the eggs for 10 minutes, then rinse thoroughly under a cold running tap until cool. Remove the shells under water and cut each egg into four. Remove the seeds from the pepper and cut into thin strips and finely chop the onion.

Arrange the beans, potatoes, eggs, peppers and onion on top of the lettuce. Add the tuna, cheese and tomatoes. Sprinkle the olives over and garnish with the basil.

To make the vinaigrette, place all the ingredients in a screw-topped jar and shake vigorously until everything is thoroughly mixed. Spoon 4 tablespoons over the top of the prepared salad and serve the remainder separately.

## FOOD FACT

Bluefin tuna is severely endangered due to overfishing. You are unlikely to find bluefin in cans, but yellowfin is also fairly overfished. Avoid both of these in preference for skipjack that is caught by rod and line. Always choose tuna steaks over chunks.

## INGREDIENTS          Serves 4

* **1 small iceberg lettuce**
* **225 g/8 oz/1½ cups French/green beans**
* **225 g/8 oz baby new potatoes, scrubbed**
* **4 eggs**
* **1 green pepper**
* **1 onion, peeled**
* **200 g/7 oz can tuna in water, drained and flaked into small pieces**
* **50 g/2 oz/½ cup low-fat hard cheese, cut into small cubes**
* **8 ripe but firm cherry tomatoes, quartered**
* **50 g/2 oz/⅓ cup black pitted olives, halved**
* **freshly chopped basil, to garnish**

### For the lime vinaigrette:

* **3 tbsp light olive oil**
* **2 tbsp white wine vinegar**
* **4 tbsp lime juice**
* **grated rind of 1 lime**
* **1 tsp Dijon mustard**
* **1–2 tsp caster/superfine sugar**
* **salt and freshly ground black pepper**

# Mediterranean Rice Salad

Rice is a definite store cupboard essential in Mediterranean countries and when added to healthy, fresh ingredients like these many delicious dishes can be prepared.

Cook the rice in a saucepan of lightly salted boiling water for 35–40 minutes, or until tender. Drain well and reserve.

Whisk the sun-dried tomatoes, garlic, oil and vinegars together in a small bowl or jug. Season to taste with salt and pepper. Put the sliced red onion in a large bowl, pour over the dressing and leave to allow the flavours to develop.

Put the peppers skin-side up on a grill/broiler rack and cook under a preheated hot grill for 5–6 minutes, or until blackened and charred. Remove and place in a polythene/plastic bag (the moisture will help loosen the skins). When cool enough to handle, peel off the skins and slice the flesh.

Add the peppers, cucumber, tomatoes, fennel and rice to the onions. Mix gently together to coat in the dressing. Cover and chill in the refrigerator for 30 minutes to allow the flavours to mingle.

Remove the salad from the refrigerator and leave to stand at room temperature for 20 minutes. Garnish with fresh basil leaves and serve.

## INGREDIENTS    Serves 4

- **250 g/9 oz/1¼ cups Camargue red rice**
- **2 sun-dried tomatoes, finely chopped**
- **2 garlic cloves, peeled and finely chopped**
- **4 tbsp oil from a jar of sun-dried tomatoes**
- **2 tsp balsamic vinegar**
- **2 tsp red wine vinegar**
- **salt and freshly ground black pepper**
- **1 red onion, peeled and thinly sliced**
- **1 yellow pepper, quartered and deseeded**
- **1 red pepper, quartered and deseeded**
- **½ cucumber, peeled and diced**
- **6 ripe plum tomatoes, cut into wedges**
- **1 fennel bulb, halved and thinly sliced**
- **fresh basil leaves, to garnish**

## FOOD FACT

Camargue red rice from the south of France is a reddish-brown colour and gives this salad a stunning appearance. It has a texture and cooking time similar to that of brown rice, which may be substituted in this recipe if Camargue red rice is unavailable.

# Quick Mediterranean Prawns

Caught in the morning and eaten in the evening, this is the healthy way the Mediterranean peoples enjoy their seafood starters and main dishes.

Remove the shells from the prawns/shrimp, leaving the tail shells. Using a small sharp knife, remove the dark vein that runs along the back of the prawns. Rinse and drain on absorbent paper towels.

Whisk 2 tablespoons of the oil with the garlic, lemon zest/rind and juice in a small bowl. Bruise 1 sprig rosemary with a rolling pin and add to the bowl. Add the prawns, toss to coat, then cover and leave to marinate in the refrigerator until needed.

For the simple dips, mix the yogurt and pesto in one bowl and the crème fraîche/sour cream, tomato paste and mustard in another bowl. Season to taste with salt and pepper.

Heat a wok, add the remaining oil and swirl round to coat the sides. Remove the prawns from the marinade, leaving any juices and the rosemary behind. Add to the wok and stir-fry over a high heat for 3–4 minutes, or until the prawns are pink and just cooked through.

Remove the prawns from the wok and arrange on a platter. Garnish with lemon wedges and more fresh rosemary sprigs and serve hot or cold with the dips.

### INGREDIENTS          Serves 4

- **20 raw Mediterranean prawns/shrimp**
- **3 tbsp olive oil**
- **1 garlic clove, peeled and crushed**
- **finely grated zest/rind and juice of ½ lemon**
- **fresh rosemary sprigs**

#### For the pesto and sun-dried tomato dips:

- **150 ml/¼ pint/⅔ cup Greek-style/plain yogurt**
- **1 tbsp prepared pesto**
- **150 ml/¼ pint/⅔ cup crème fraîche/sour cream**
- **1 tbsp sun-dried tomato paste**
- **1 tbsp wholegrain mustard**
- **salt and freshly ground black pepper**
- **lemon wedges, to garnish**

### HELPFUL HINT

The prawns must be cooked thoroughly, but take care not to overcook them or they will be tough.
Remove from the refrigerator and leave at room temperature for 15 minutes before stir-frying.

# Griddled Garlic & Lemon Squid

Searching for squid in the rocks is a pastime undertaken by many a Mediterranean youth; not surprising if they get to eat this tasty dish.

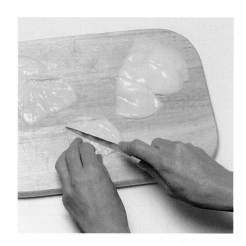

Rinse the rice until the water runs clear, then place in a saucepan with the stock.

Bring to the boil, then reduce the heat. Cover and simmer gently for 10 minutes.

Turn off the heat and leave the pan covered so the rice can steam while you cook the squid.

Remove the tentacles from the squid and reserve.

Cut the body cavity in half. Using the tip of a small sharp knife, score the inside flesh of the body cavity in a diamond pattern. Do not cut all the way through.

Mix the lemon zest/rind, crushed garlic and chopped shallot together.

Place the squid in a shallow bowl and sprinkle over the lemon mixture and stir.

Heat a griddle pan until almost smoking. Cook the squid for 3–4 minutes until cooked through, then slice.

Sprinkle with the coriander/cilantro and lemon juice. Season to taste with salt and pepper. Drain the rice and serve immediately with the squid.

## INGREDIENTS        Serves 4

- **125 g/4 oz/⅔ cup long-grain rice**
- **300 ml/½ pint/1¼ cups fish stock**
- **225 g/8 oz squid, cleaned**
- **finely grated zest/rind of 1 lemon**
- **1 garlic clove, peeled and crushed**
- **1 shallot, peeled and finely chopped**
- **2 tbsp freshly chopped coriander/cilantro**
- **2 tbsp lemon juice**
- **salt and freshly ground black pepper**

## HELPFUL HINT

To prepare squid, peel the tentacles from the squid's pouch and cut away the header just below the eye. Discard the header. Remove the quill and the soft innards from the squid and discard. Peel off any dark skin that covers the squid and discard. Rinse the tentacles and pouch thoroughly. The squid is now ready to use.

# Eastern Europe

Like all Mediterranean cuisine, the freshness of the ingredients is key to meals prepared in Europe's Eastern Mediterranean countries.

# Greece, Crete & Cyprus

Greek food has evolved over the centuries, influenced by the numerous invasions the country has suffered at the hands of the Minoans, the Romans, the Byzantines, the Italians, the Arabs and the Turks. But there are still some dishes that can be traced back to the Ancient Greeks, involving ingredients such as nuts, garlic, olive oil, lemons, sesame, honey, cheeses and dried meats. Natural, grown locally, freshly picked and cooked on the same day are all important elements of Greek cuisine.

Scattered around the eastern Mediterranean, Greece's islands are sun-kissed with a temperate climate. This provides the country with an abundance of fresh vegetables, fruits and herbs to use in their excellent cuisine. In addition, most of Greece is less than 130 km (80 miles) from the Mediterranean Sea, so fish plays an important role in its cuisine too. Kalamari, or squid, is served as a starter or a main course and this can be griddled with lemon or fried in batter. Fish roe dip, or taramasalata, can form part of a Greek mezethes (a selection of snacks rather like tapas), along with tzatziki (cucumber and yogurt dip) or aubergine dip.

The lushness of the slopes of the many mountainous regions throughout Greece enable the sheep and goats living on them to thrive. The Greeks eat the meat and use the milk of these animals to make feta cheese, which is used in their salads, along with olives, which grow in abundance in the country, most famously on the island of Crete. Cheese and spinach pies, or simply cheese pies, are made from feta or other local cheeses, using filo pastry and offered to guests or eaten as a starter or main dish accompanied by a salad.

Because Greece comprises such a large number of smaller islands in addition to its mainland, the country's recipes are extremely diverse – each of the islands has its own way of selecting and preparing the ingredients. Many of the islands also have their own specialities, normally based around their success

at growing one of the ingredients locally. Greek cooking is very frugal; and the Greeks tend to cook whatever they have available in the garden, so dishes are seasonal, and when fresh food is not available they turn to dried foods. Little use is made of a freezer in Greece.

Lamb plays an important role in Greek food and is often served as a celebration dish. It is spit roasted, slow roasted in the oven, stewed or casseroled. Minced lamb is used in moussaka, together with sliced aubergine, garlic, onion and béchamel sauce topped with grated cheese. Minced lamb can also be added to the small, new leaves of the grapevine, along with rice and herbs, to make dolmades, or stuffed vine leaves.

Crete (pictured right) is the largest of the Greek islands. It sits in the centre of the eastern Mediterranean basin, where the continents of Europe, Asia and Africa meet. Crete has one of the oldest cuisine traditions in the world; tastes, smells, ingredients and skills have all survived from prehistoric times. Their diet is rich in vegetables, pulses, fruits, cereals, salads, fish and grilled meat and their major source of fat is olive oil: very little butter is used for cooking. They season their food with herbs and make their sesame-topped bread with yeast. They also eat mountain snails, which can be cooked in a number of different ways.

The value of honey has been appreciated in Crete since ancient times. In the Egyptian Papyruses, honey is mentioned as a healing treatment and the ancient Indians claimed that drinking honey and milk daily would preserve and prolong life. In Greek mythology Zeus was raised on honey from the nymph bee and both Hippocrates and Aristotle recommended honey for the healing of many illnesses. The Egyptians offered honeycombs to their gods as a precious gift of loyalty and consolation.

Greek recipes in general have been strongly influenced by Turkish and Middle Eastern cuisine and as an independent island Crete is self-sufficient in year-round fresh fruit and vegetables, as well as in seafood. Cretan specialities are the local Graviera cheese (much like Gruyère) and Myzithra, a creamy white cheese that is often served instead of feta cheese in Greek salads.

Determined by the seasons, dishes are cooked with what is available. By October the grapes have been picked and dried, so sweet recipes involve sultanas and the wholesome sweet dish called mustalevriá, which is made from the leftovers of the grape pressing and winemaking. In November the walnuts are ready and dishes are made combining these with honey and yogurt. Then the oranges are ready by January and many Cretan housewives preserve them to make gliká tou koutalioú, which literally transcribes to 'sweet of the spoon', a process much like jam-making. The sugar preserves the fruit, which can also be figs, apricots, cherries, quince and grapes and these treats are kept in the store cupboard to offer to guests with their coffee.

Another Cretan staple is a dried, rusk-like bread that is traditionally made throughout Greece with barley or whole meal. It is sliced three quarters of the way through before being baked. These dákos can be broken into chunks and added to a Greek salad, or they can be used to make a well-known Greek dish also called dákos. The rusks are drizzled with water and olive oil to soften them and tomatoes are grated on top of the dried slices. Salt, pepper, olive oil and feta cheese are used to top the dákos, together with green or black olives.

Cyprus (pictured right), a former British colony, is the third largest island in the Mediterranean Sea. In 1974 it was invaded by the Turks, who successfully occupied a third of the island's land, in the north. Cuisine in the non-Turkish southern areas of Cyprus is traditionally Greek, but with the expected island-specific slant. Halloumi cheese is a speciality of Cyprus and is made from a mixture of goat's and sheep's milk with mint leaves. Usually grilled as an appetizer, sometimes with Lountza, a Cypriot ham, the method for making this cheese originated in Cyprus. Other traditional Cypriot dishes

centre around the fresh produce and the fruit of the sea. Squid, octopus, sea bass and red mullet are all used regularly in dishes, as are salads and vegetables, which are also pickled to preserve them.

Cypriot meat specialities include sheftalia, which is minced meat that has been moulded into a sausage-shape and wrapped in the intestines of the animal. Most Cypriot meat is marinated before cooking, often in olive oil, wine, lemon juice and dried coriander. Bulgur wheat is used regularly in Cypriot recipes, as are nuts, artichokes and fresh figs.

Throughout Greece and Cyprus the small, hot or cold, fish, vegetable, meat or fruit dishes make up the mezethes or meze. Originally served by housewives to their guests, these meze were literally whatever was left in the kitchen. The small dishes are served with drinks, whether it is wine (Krasomezethes) or a glass of the fiery Greek Ouzo (Ouzomezethes). Greek eating is all about company. Because of the temperate climate the Greeks tend to eat late at night and to entertain guests often and it never matters if unexpected guests arrive; the Greek housewife can always compile an ad hoc meze to offer them.

# Albania

Situated between Greece, Macedonia, Kosovo and Montenegro, like most of the countries that border the Mediterranean, Albania's cuisine has been influenced over the years by the occupation of other countries. Greece, Italy and the Ottoman Turks all occupied Albania and each has left its mark on their cuisine; over the years Albania has accumulated styles from the Balkan as well as Mediterranean nations.

Before this, Albania's different regions had their own unique styles of cooking, but Communist rule obliterated these separate identities and now their recipes are countrywide.

Albania's vegetation is rich and their recipes combine ingredients with spices, oregano, olives and grapes. Seafood specialities are common in the coastal areas of Durrës, Vlorë

and Sarandë. Albania's mild climate favours agriculture so they grow and cook peppers, aubergines, tomatoes, cucumbers and vegetables. These are used with meats and fish to form dishes often baked in earthenware pots or sautéed to make stews, casseroles, stuffed vegetables or meatballs.

garlic and hot peppers are popular, as are lemons, vinegar and yogurt, although these are added by taste rather than following recipes. Many Albanians make and consume yogurt daily, together with buttermilk; these two ingredients are used countrywide as the basis for sauces and other dishes.

Olives are a staple and are grown in Berat, Vlora, Borsh, Himara and Tirana. Frequently these are eaten alone, or as part of a meze, but are often combined with meats and vegetables as an essential ingredient in traditional Albanian dishes. Albanians also use a variety of spices to enhance the flavour;

Albanian cheeses still tend to vary by region, with the most popular countrywide a white cheese made from sheep's milk. This originated in the south of Albania and is similar to Greek feta cheese and similarly added to home-grown salads.

# The South Slavic Countries

**Slovenia, Croatia, Bosnia and Herzegovina and Montenegro were all parts of the former Republic of Yugoslavia until 1992; each country borders the Mediterranean Sea. Unsurprisingly, it is the coastal areas of these countries that are more typically 'Mediterranean' food-wise.**

With a varied terrain and climate, Slovenian cuisine varies from region to region. Many base their dishes on bacon, lard, dripping, mushrooms, pork, flour-based dishes, potatoes, beans, butter, cream and eggs. Others include porridge, stew and one-pot meals, like soups from turnip peel or beef and chicken soups,

The Mediterranean provides the coastal regions with squid, cuttlefish, tuna, shrimps, mussels, cod, clams and lobster, whilst others specialize in soups, stews, pasta, spicy garlic sausages and ham, sheep's, goat's and curd cheese and salty pies, like Dalmatian vegetable pie. The Viennese-influence shows in the pastries and cakes, such as strudel with apple and cheese filling.

The food of Bosnia (pictured left below) is influenced by the Turkish, Greeks and Central Europe. They use moderate spices and cook their food in plenty of water with tomatoes, potatoes, onions, garlic and peppers. Fresh vegetables are used regularly. Beef and lamb, with some pork, are eaten; pilaf and goulash are popular meals and dessert recipes originate from Greece and Turkey.

served on special occasions. Kettle goulash (bogracs gulyas), a Slovenian one-pot meal, uses bacon fat, onions, green peppers, garlic, paprika, stewing beef, tomato paste, sour cream and seasoning. The dishes from Bela Krajina and Primorska are based around mutton and goat's meat or poultry, whilst in Dolenjska and Notranjska they eat roasted dormouse, quail and hedgehog.

The inner regions of Croatia have been influenced over the years by the Turks, Hungarians and Viennese; and the Mediterranean regions (pictured above) by the Greeks, Romans, Italians and French in their cuisine. Known as the 'cuisine of the regions', Croatian ingredients and recipes come from its varied regions.

The food of Montenegro (pictured right) is distinctively Italian, particularly its bread-making style, meat curing and drying, cheese making, soups and stews, polenta, stuffed capsicums and love of meatballs. However they also serve moussaka, pitta, kebab and Hungarian goulash, whilst for dessert they enjoy baklava and crepes.

Mediterran

# Meat & Fish

Many countries that border the Mediterranean Sea will have their own version of the recipes shown in this section of the book, particularly those that the sea itself provides them with.

The terrain, the lushness of the vegetation and several other factors will determine how well or otherwise the country's locals are at rearing and breeding livestock. Goat and lamb are virtually impossible to distinguish from one another flavour-wise when they are cooked well. In many cases goat can be substituted for lamb when it is not available or when it is too expensive, for example in Lamb and Potato Moussaka.

# Lamb & Potato Moussaka

This recipe replaces the more traditional béchamel sauce topping with the healthier option of blending together yogurt, cheese and eggs.

Preheat the oven to 200°C/400°F/Gas Mark 6, about 15 minutes before required. Thinly slice the potatoes and rinse thoroughly in cold water, then pat dry with a clean dishtowel.

Melt 50 g/2 oz/¼ stick of the butter in a frying pan and fry the potatoes, in batches, until crisp and golden. Using a slotted spoon, remove from the pan and reserve. Use one third of the potatoes to line the base of an ovenproof dish.

Add the onion and garlic to the butter remaining in the pan and cook for 5 minutes. Add the lamb and fry for 1 minute. Blend the tomato puree/paste with 3 tablespoons water and stir into the pan with the parsley and salt and pepper. Spoon over the layer of potatoes, then top with the remaining potato slices.

Heat the oil and the remaining butter in the pan and brown the aubergine/eggplant slices for 5–6 minutes. Arrange the tomatoes on top of the potatoes, then the aubergines on top of the tomatoes. Beat the eggs with the yogurt and Parmesan cheese. Pour over the aubergine and tomatoes. Bake in the preheated oven for 25 minutes, or until golden and piping hot. Serve.

## INGREDIENTS    Serves 4

- **4–6 potatoes, peeled**
- **125 g/4½ oz/1 stick plus 1 tbsp butter**
- **1 large onion, peeled and chopped**
- **2–4 garlic cloves, peeled and crushed**
- **700 g/1½ lb cooked roast lamb, trimmed and cubed**
- **3 tbsp tomato puree/paste**
- **1 tbsp freshly chopped parsley**
- **salt and freshly ground black pepper**
- **3–4 tbsp olive oil**
- **2 aubergines/eggplants, trimmed and sliced**
- **4 tomatoes, sliced**
- **2 eggs**
- **300 ml/½ pint/1¼ cups Greek/plain yogurt**
- **2–3 tbsp grated Parmesan cheese**

## HELPFUL HINT

It is worth salting the aubergines to ensure that any bitterness is removed. Layer the slices in a colander, sprinkling a little salt between the layers. Leave for 20 minutes, then rinse under cold running water and pat dry on absorbent paper towels. Salting helps the aubergines to absorb less oil when frying.

# Chicken Chasseur

French in origin, this recipe is used throughout many Mediterranean Sea coastal regions, although each may have its own variation.

Preheat the oven to 180°C/350°F/Gas Mark 4. Skin the chicken, if preferred, and rinse lightly. Pat dry on absorbent paper towels. Heat the oil and butter in an ovenproof casserole (or frying pan, if preferred), add the chicken portions and cook, in batches, until browned all over. Remove with a slotted spoon and reserve.

Add the onions, garlic and celery to the casserole and cook for 5 minutes, or until golden. Cut the mushrooms in half if large, then add to the casserole and cook for 2 minutes.

Sprinkle in the flour and cook for 2 minutes, then gradually stir in the wine. Blend the tomato puree/paste with a little of the stock in a small bowl, then stir into the casserole together with the remaining stock. Bring to the boil, stirring constantly.

If a frying pan has been used, transfer everything to a casserole. Return the chicken to the casserole, season to taste and add a few tarragon sprigs.

Stir in the sweet potato, cover with a lid and cook in the oven for 30 minutes. Remove the casserole from the oven and add the broad/fava beans. Return to the oven and cook for a further 15–20 minutes, or until the chicken and vegetables are cooked. Serve sprinkled with chopped tarragon.

## INGREDIENTS    Serves 4

- **1 whole chicken, about 1.5 kg/3 lb in weight, jointed into 4 or 8 portions**
- **1 tbsp olive oil**
- **1 tbsp unsalted butter**
- **12 baby onions, peeled**
- **2–4 garlic cloves, peeled and sliced**
- **2 celery stalks, trimmed and sliced**
- **175 g/6 oz/1¾ cups closed cup mushrooms, wiped**
- **2 tbsp plain/all-purpose flour**
- **300 ml/½ pint/1¼ cups dry white wine**
- **2 tbsp tomato puree/paste**
- **450 ml/¾ pint/1¾ cups chicken stock**
- **salt and freshly ground black pepper**
- **few sprigs fresh tarragon**
- **350 g/12 oz/2⅔ cups sweet potatoes, peeled and cut into chunks**
- **300 g/10 oz/2 cups shelled fresh or frozen broad/fava beans**
- **1 tbsp freshly chopped tarragon, to garnish**

# Cassoulet

This rich meaty bean stew or casserole is cooked very slowly; it originated in the south of France.

Preheat the oven to 180°C/350°F/Gas Mark 4. Heat the oil in a large saucepan or ovenproof casserole, add the onion, celery, carrot and garlic and sauté for 5 minutes. Cut the pork, if using, into small pieces and cut the sausages into chunks.

Add the meat to the vegetables and cook, stirring, until lightly browned.

Add the thyme sprigs and season to taste with salt and pepper. If a saucepan was used, transfer everything to an ovenproof casserole.

Spoon the beans on top, then pour in the stock. Mix the breadcrumbs with 1 tablespoon of the chopped thyme in a small bowl and sprinkle on top of the beans. Cover with a lid and cook in the oven for 40 minutes. Remove the lid and cook for a further 15 minutes, or until the breadcrumbs are crisp. Sprinkle with the remaining chopped thyme and serve.

## INGREDIENTS        Serves 4

- **1 tbsp olive oil**
- **1 onion, peeled and chopped**
- **2 celery stalks, trimmed and chopped**
- **175 g/6 oz /1½ cups carrots, peeled and sliced**
- **2–3 garlic cloves, peeled and crushed**
- **350 g/12 oz pork belly (optional)**
- **8 spicy thick sausages, such as Toulouse**
- **few fresh thyme sprigs**
- **salt and freshly ground black pepper**
- **2 x 400 g/14 oz cans cannellini beans, drained and rinsed**
- **600 ml/1 pint/2½ cups vegetable stock**
- **75 g/3 oz/1½ cups fresh breadcrumbs**
- **2 tbsp freshly chopped thyme**

## TASTY TIP

Replace the pork belly with lardons/fatty bacon chunks, if you prefer.

# Spanish-style Pork Stew and Saffron Rice

The simple addition of a few strands of saffron makes this delicious dish even more attractive when it is served.

Preheat the oven to 150°C/300°F/Gas Mark 2. Heat the oil in a large flameproof casserole and add the pork in batches. Fry over a high heat until browned. Transfer to a plate until all the pork is browned.

Lower the heat and add the onion to the casserole. Cook for a further 5 minutes until soft and starting to brown. Add the garlic and stir briefly before returning the pork to the casserole. Add the flour and stir.

Add the tomatoes. Gradually stir in the red wine and add the basil. Bring to simmering point and cover. Transfer the casserole to the lower part of the preheated oven and cook for 1½ hours. Stir in the green pepper and olives and cook for 30 minutes. Season to taste with salt and pepper.

Meanwhile, to make the saffron rice, heat the oil with the butter in a saucepan. Add the onion and cook for 5 minutes over a medium heat until softened. Add the saffron and rice and stir well. Add the stock, bring to the boil, cover and reduce the heat as low as possible. Cook for 15 minutes, covered, until the rice is tender and the stock is absorbed. Adjust the seasoning and serve with the stew, garnished with fresh basil.

## INGREDIENTS    Serves 4

- **2 tbsp olive oil**
- **900 g/2 lb boneless pork shoulder, diced**
- **1 large onion, peeled and sliced**
- **2 garlic cloves, peeled and finely chopped**
- **1 tbsp plain/all-purpose flour**
- **450 g/1 lb plum tomatoes, peeled and chopped**
- **175 ml/6 fl oz/scant ¾ cup red wine**
- **1 tbsp freshly chopped basil**
- **1 green pepper, deseeded and sliced**
- **50 g/2 oz/½ cup pimiento-stuffed olives, cut in half crossways**
- **salt and freshly ground black pepper**
- **fresh basil leaves, to garnish**

### For the saffron rice:
- **1 tbsp olive oil**
- **25 g/1 oz/¼ stick butter**
- **1 small onion, peeled and finely chopped**
- **few strands saffron, crushed**
- **250 g/9 oz/1⅓ cups long-grain white rice**
- **600 ml/1 pint/2½ cups chicken stock**

# Chicken with Roasted Fennel & Citrus Rice

The aromatic ingredients in this recipe are so representative of the dishes of many of the countries bordering the Mediterranean.

Preheat the oven to 200°C/400°F/Gas Mark 6. Lightly crush the fennel seeds and mix with oregano, garlic, salt and pepper. Place between the skin and flesh of the chicken breasts, careful not to tear the skin. Arrange the lemon slices on top of the chicken.

Cut the fennel into eight wedges. Place on baking tray with the chicken. Lightly brush the fennel with the oil. Cook the chicken and fennel on the top shelf of the preheated oven for 10 minutes.

Meanwhile, put the rice in a 2.3 litre/4 pint/2¼ quart ovenproof dish. Stir in the lemon zest/rind and juice, orange juice and stock. Cover with a lid and put on the middle shelf of the oven. Reduce the oven temperature to 180°C/350°F/Gas Mark 4. Cook the chicken for a further 40 minutes, turning the fennel wedges and lemon slices once.

Deseed and chop the tomatoes. Add to the tray with the chicken and cook for 5–10 minutes. Remove from the oven.

When cooled slightly, remove the chicken skin and discard. Fluff the rice, scatter olives over the dish. Garnish with fennel fronds and orange slices and serve.

## INGREDIENTS          Serves 4

- **2 tsp fennel seeds**
- **1 tbsp freshly chopped oregano**
- **1 garlic clove, peeled and crushed**
- **salt and freshly ground black pepper**
- **4 chicken quarters, about 175 g/6 oz each**
- **½ lemon, finely sliced**
- **1 fennel bulb, trimmed**
- **2 tsp olive oil**
- **4 plum tomatoes**
- **25 g/1 oz/¼ cup pitted green olives**

### To garnish:
- **fennel fronds**
- **orange slices**

### For the citrus rice:
- **225 g/8 oz/1¼ cup long-grain rice**
- **finely grated zest/rind and juice of ½ lemon**
- **150 ml/¼ pint/⅔ cup orange juice**
- **450 ml/¾ pint/1¾ cups boiling chicken or vegetable stock**

# Spicy Chicken Skewers with Mango Tabbouleh

Used in Turkish, Greek and Albanian recipes, bulgur wheat is made from durum wheat and has a light, nutty flavour.

If using wooden skewers, pre-soak them in cold water for at least 30 minutes. (This stops them from burning during grilling.) Cut the chicken into 5 × 1 cm/2 × ½ inch strips and place in a shallow dish.

Mix together the yogurt, garlic, chilli, turmeric, lemon zest/rind and juice. Pour over the chicken and toss to coat. Cover and leave to marinate in the refrigerator for up to 8 hours.

To make the tabbouleh, put the bulgur wheat in a bowl. Pour over enough boiling water to cover. Put a plate over the bowl. Leave to soak for 20 minutes.

Whisk together the oil and lemon juice in a bowl. Add the red onion and leave to marinate for 10 minutes.

Drain the bulgur wheat and squeeze out any excess moisture in a clean dishtowel. Add to the red onion with the mango, cucumber and herbs and season to taste with salt and pepper. Toss together.

Thread the chicken strips onto 8 wooden or metal skewers. Cook under a hot grill/broiler for 8 minutes. Turn and brush with the marinade, until the chicken is lightly browned and cooked through. Spoon the tabbouleh onto individual plates. Arrange the chicken skewers on top and garnish with the mint sprigs. Serve warm or cold.

## INGREDIENTS    Serves 4

- **400 g/14 oz chicken breast fillet**
- **200 ml/7 fl oz/¾ cup natural/plain low-fat yogurt**
- **1 garlic clove, peeled and crushed**
- **1 small red chilli, deseeded and finely chopped**
- **½ tsp ground turmeric**
- **finely grated zest/rind and juice of ½ lemon**
- **fresh mint sprigs, to garnish**

### For the mango tabbouleh:
- **175 g/6 oz/1 cup bulgur wheat**
- **1 tsp olive oil**
- **juice of ½ lemon**
- **½ red onion, finely chopped**
- **1 ripe mango, halved, stoned, peeled and chopped**
- **¼ cucumber, finely diced**
- **2 tbsp freshly chopped parsley**
- **2 tbsp freshly shredded mint**
- **salt and finely ground black pepper**

# Moroccan Lamb with Apricots

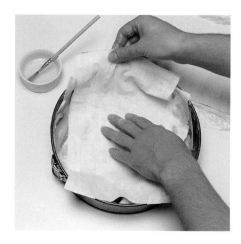

The careful use of cardamom, ginger and cumin make this a very tempting, mouth-wateringly aromatic dish whilst it is slowly cooking.

Preheat the oven to 190°C/375°F/Gas Mark 5. Pound the ginger, garlic, cardamom and cumin to a paste with a pestle and mortar. Heat 1 tablespoon of the oil in a large frying pan and fry the spice paste for 3 minutes. Remove and reserve.

Add the remaining oil and fry the lamb in batches for about 5 minutes until golden brown. Return all the lamb to the pan and add the onions and spice paste. Fry for 10 minutes, stirring occasionally.

Add the chopped tomatoes, cover and simmer for 15 minutes. Add the apricots and chickpeas and simmer for a further 15 minutes.

Lightly oil a round 18 cm/7 inch spring-form cake tin/pan. Lay one sheet of pastry dough in the base of the tin, allowing the excess to fall over the sides. Brush with melted butter, then layer five more sheets in the tin and brush each one with butter.

Spoon in the filling and level the surface. Layer half the remaining dough sheets on top, again brushing each with butter. Fold the overhanging pastry over the top of the filling. Brush the remaining sheet with butter and scrunch up and place on top of the pie so that the whole pie is completely covered. Brush with melted butter once more.

Bake in the preheated oven for 45 minutes, then reserve for 10 minutes. Unclip the tin and remove the pie. Sprinkle with the nutmeg, garnish with the dill sprigs and serve.

## INGREDIENTS          Serves 6

- **5 cm/2 inch piece root ginger, peeled and grated**
- **3 garlic cloves, peeled and crushed**
- **1 tsp ground cardamom**
- **1 tsp ground cumin**
- **2 tbsp olive oil**
- **450 g/1 lb lamb neck fillet, cubed**
- **1 large red onion, peeled and chopped**
- **400 g/14 oz can chopped tomatoes**
- **125 g/4 oz ready-to-eat dried apricots**
- **400 g/14 oz can chickpeas, drained**
- **7 large sheets filo/phyllo pastry dough**
- **50 g/2 oz/½ stick butter, melted**
- **pinch nutmeg**
- **dill sprigs, to garnish**

# Bouillabaisse

Originating from the Provençal port city of Marseille, this fish stew is delicately flavoured with herbs, spices and vegetables.

Cut the fish into thick pieces, peel the prawns/shrimp if necessary and rinse well. Place the saffron strands in a small bowl, cover with warm water and leave to infuse for at least 10 minutes.

Heat the oil in a large heavy-based saucepan or casserole, add the onions and celery and fry for 5 minutes, stirring occasionally. Add the tomatoes, bay leaf, garlic and bouquet garni and stir until lightly coated with the oil.

Place the firm fish on top of the tomatoes and pour in the saffron-infused water and enough water to just cover. Bring to the boil, reduce the heat, cover with a lid and cook for 8 minutes.

Add the soft-flesh fish and continue to simmer for 5 minutes, or until all the fish are cooked. Season to taste with salt and pepper, remove and discard the bouquet garni and serve with French bread.

## INGREDIENTS    Serves 4–6

- **675 g/1½ lb assorted fish, such as whiting, mackerel, red mullet, salmon and king prawns/jumbo shrimp, cleaned and skinned**
- **few saffron strands**
- **3 tbsp olive oil**
- **2 onions, peeled and sliced**
- **2 celery stalks, trimmed and sliced**
- **225 g/8 oz/1¼ cups ripe tomatoes, peeled and chopped**
- **1 fresh bay leaf**
- **2–3 garlic cloves, peeled and crushed**
- **1 bouquet garni**
- **sea salt and freshly ground black pepper**
- **French bread, to serve**

## TASTY TIP

Traditionally, eight different fish are used for this dish. Use as many as you wish, but make sure you remove as many bones as possible and use fresh not smoked fish. If liked, use fish stock in place of the water – you will need about 600–750 ml/1–1¼ pints/2½–3¼ cups.

# Ratatouille Mackerel

This versatile and tasty French dish gives the cook a number of different options for substituting individual vegetables for variety.

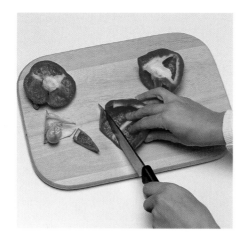

Preheat the oven to 190°C/375°F/Gas Mark 5. Cut the top off the red pepper, remove the seeds and membrane, then cut into chunks. Cut the red onion into thick wedges.

Heat the oil in a large pan and cook the onion and garlic for 5 minutes, or until beginning to soften.

Add the pepper chunks and courgette/zucchini slices and cook for a further 5 minutes.

Pour in the chopped tomatoes with their juice and cook for a further 5 minutes. Season to taste with salt and pepper and pour into an ovenproof dish.

Season the fish with salt and pepper and arrange on top of the vegetables. Spray with a little olive oil and lemon juice. Cover and cook in the preheated oven for 20 minutes.

Remove the cover, add the basil leaves and return to the oven for a further 5 minutes. Serve immediately with couscous or rice mixed with parsley.

## INGREDIENTS        Serves 4

- **1 red pepper**
- **1 white or red onion, peeled**
- **1 tbsp olive oil**
- **1 garlic clove, peeled and thinly sliced**
- **2 courgettes/zucchini, trimmed and cut into thick slices**
- **400 g/14 oz can chopped tomatoes**
- **sea salt and freshly ground black pepper**
- **4 x 275 g/10 oz small mackerel, cleaned and heads removed**
- **spray of olive oil**
- **lemon juice, for drizzling**
- **12 fresh basil leaves**
- **couscous or rice mixed with chopped parsley, to serve**

## TASTY TIP

For that extra kick, why not add a little chopped chilli?

# Potato Boulangère with Sea Bass

Boulangère is a classic French dish. Sea bass is traditionally caught and cooked in the southern Slavic countries, although it is enjoyed throughout the Mediterranean countries.

Preheat the oven to 200°C/400°F/Gas Mark 6. Lightly grease a shallow 1.4 litre/2½ pint/1½ quart baking dish with oil or butter. Layer the potato slices and onions alternately in the prepared dish, seasoning each layer with salt and pepper.

Pour the stock over the top, then cut 50 g/2 oz/4 tbsp of the butter or margarine into small pieces and dot over the top layer. Bake in the preheated oven for 50–60 minutes. Do not cover the dish at this stage.

Lightly rinse the sea bass fillets and pat dry on absorbent paper towels. Cook in a griddle, or heat the remaining butter or margarine in a frying pan and shallow fry the fish fillets for 3–4 minutes per side, flesh side first. Remove from the pan with a slotted spatula and drain on absorbent paper towels.

Remove the partly cooked potato and onion mixture from the oven and place the fish on the top. Cover with kitchen foil and return to the oven for 10 minutes until heated through. Garnish with sprigs of parsley and serve immediately.

## INGREDIENTS     Serves 2

- **450 g/1 lb potatoes, peeled and thinly sliced**
- **1 large onion, peeled and thinly sliced**
- **salt and freshly ground black pepper**
- **300 ml/½ pint/1¼ cups fish or vegetable stock**
- **75 g/3 oz/⅓ stick butter or margarine**
- **350 g/12 oz sea bass fillets**
- **fresh flat-leaf/Italian parsley sprigs, to garnish**

## FOOD FACT

Sea bass, also known as sea perch, is a large round fish which grows up to 1 m/3⅓ ft long, and may weigh up to 9 kg/20 lb. In appearance, it is similar to a salmon, but a much darker grey colour. Cook it gently and handle it with care, as the flesh is soft and delicate.

# Seared Tuna with Pernod & Thyme

French Pernod and thyme are a classic combination that can be used with other fish, like swordfish or shark steaks.

Wipe the fish steaks with a damp cloth or dampened paper towels.

Season both sides of the fish to taste with salt and pepper, then place in a shallow bowl and reserve.

Mix together the Pernod, olive oil, lime zest and juice with the fresh thyme leaves.

Finely chop the sun-dried tomatoes and add to the Pernod mixture.

Pour the Pernod mixture over the fish and chill in the refrigerator for about 2 hours, occasionally spooning the marinade over the fish.

Heat a griddle or heavy-based frying pan. Drain the fish, reserving the marinade. Cook the fish for 3–4 minutes on each side for a steak that is still slightly pink in the middle. Or, if liked, cook the fish for 1–2 minutes longer on each side if you prefer your fish cooked through.

Place the remaining marinade in a small saucepan and bring to the boil. Pour the marinade over the fish and serve immediately, with the mixed rice and salad.

## INGREDIENTS    Serves 4

- **4 tuna or swordfish steaks**
- **salt and freshly ground black pepper**
- **3 tbsp Pernod**
- **1 tbsp olive oil**
- **zest and juice of 1 lime**
- **2 tsp fresh thyme leaves**
- **4 sun-dried tomatoes**

### To serve:
- **freshly cooked mixed rice**
- **tossed green salad**

## FOOD FACT

Fresh tuna is an oily fish rich in Omega-3 fatty acids which help in the prevention of heart disease by lowering blood cholesterol levels. Tuna is usually sold in steaks, and the flesh should be dark red in colour.

# Seared Pancetta-wrapped Cod

Pancetta is Italian-cured belly pork, which is often delicately smoked. Slices of pancetta are often used as below to encase poultry or fish.

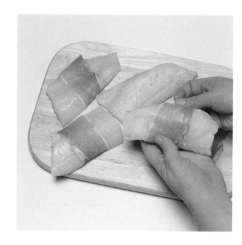

Wipe the cod fillets and wrap each one with the pancetta. Secure each fillet with a cocktail stick/toothpick and reserve.

Drain the capers and soak in cold water for 10 minutes to remove any excess salt, then drain and reserve.

Heat the oil in a large frying pan and sear the wrapped pieces of cod fillet for about 3 minutes on each side, turning carefully with a fish slice so as not to break up the fish. Lower the heat, then continue to cook for 2–3 minutes, or until the fish is thoroughly cooked.

Meanwhile, place the reserved capers, lemon juice and olive oil into a small saucepan. Grind over some black pepper.

Place the saucepan over a low heat and bring to a gentle simmer, stirring continuously, for 2–3 minutes.

Once the fish is cooked, garnish with the parsley and serve with the warm caper dressing, freshly cooked vegetables and new potatoes.

## INGREDIENTS    Serves 4

- **4 x 175 g/6 oz thick cod fillets**
- **4 very thin slices pancetta**
- **3 tbsp capers in vinegar**
- **1 tbsp vegetable or sunflower/corn oil**
- **2 tbsp lemon juice**
- **1 tbsp olive oil**
- **freshly ground black pepper**
- **1 tbsp freshly chopped parsley, to garnish**

**To serve:**
- **freshly cooked vegetables**
- **freshly cooked new potatoes**

## FOOD FACT

Chopped pancetta is often used in sauces. To cook chopped pancetta, fry for 2–3 minutes and reserve. Use the oil to seal meat or to fry onions, then return the pancetta to the pan.

# Mussels Linguine

The flatter variety of pasta noodles, linguine are popularly served with light-textured sauces and seafood, such as here in this classic Italian dish.

Soak the mussels in plenty of cold water. Leave in the refrigerator until required. When ready to use, scrub the mussel shells, removing any barnacles or beards. Discard any open mussels.

Melt the butter in a large pan. Add the mussels, onion and wine. Cover with a close-fitting lid and steam for 5–6 minutes, shaking the pan gently to ensure even cooking. Discard any mussels that have not opened, then strain and reserve the liquor.

To make the sauce, heat the oil in a medium-sized saucepan and gently fry the quartered onion and garlic for 3–4 minutes until soft and transparent. Stir in the tomatoes and half the reserved mussel liquor. Bring to the boil and simmer for 7–10 minutes until the sauce begins to thicken.

Cook the pasta in boiling salted water for 7 minutes or until *al dente*. Drain the pasta, reserving 2 tablespoons of the cooking liquor, then return the pasta and liquor to the pan.

Remove the meat from half the mussel shells. Stir into the sauce along with the remaining mussels. Pour the hot sauce over the cooked pasta and toss gently. Garnish with the parsley and serve immediately.

## INGREDIENTS    Serves 4

- **2 kg/4½ lb fresh mussels, washed and scrubbed**
- **knob butter**
- **1 onion, peeled and finely chopped**
- **300 ml/½ pint/1¼ cups medium dry white wine**

### For the sauce:
- **1 tbsp sunflower oil**
- **4 baby onions, peeled and quartered**
- **2 garlic cloves, peeled and crushed**
- **400 g/14 oz can chopped tomatoes**
- **large pinch salt**
- **225 g/8 oz dried linguine or tagliatelle**
- **2 tbsp freshly chopped parsley**

## TASTY TIP

Serving mussels in their shells is a fantastic way to eat them. Every mussel is surrounded with the delicious sauce, adding flavour to every mouthful. Clams, which often have a sweeter flavour, could also be used in this recipe.

# Seafood Risotto

Italian Arborio rice is a short-grain rice variety that grows in the Po Valley and is excellent in all risotto dishes.

Melt the butter in a large heavy-based saucepan, add the shallots and garlic and cook for 2 minutes until slightly softened. Add the rice and cook for 1–2 minutes, stirring continuously, then pour in the wine and boil for 1 minute.

Pour in half the hot stock, bring to the boil, cover the saucepan and simmer gently for 15 minutes, adding the remaining stock a little at a time. Continue to simmer for 5 minutes, or until the rice is cooked and all the liquid is absorbed.

Meanwhile, prepare the fish by peeling the prawns/shrimp and removing the headers and tails. Drain the clams and discard the liquid. Cut the smoked salmon trimmings into thin strips.

When the rice has cooked, stir in the prawns, smoked salmon strips, clams and half the chopped parsley, then heat through for 1–2 minutes until everything is piping hot. Turn into a serving dish, sprinkle with the remaining parsley and the Parmesan cheese and serve immediately with a green salad and crusty bread.

## INGREDIENTS          Serves 4

- **50 g/2 oz/½ stick butter**
- **2 shallots, peeled and finely chopped**
- **1 garlic clove, peeled and crushed**
- **350 g/12 oz/2 cups Arborio/risotto rice**
- **150 ml/¼ pint/⅔ cup white wine**
- **600 ml/1 pint/2½ cups fish or vegetable stock, heated**
- **125 g/4½ oz/¾ cup large prawns/shrimp**
- **50 g/2 oz/½ cup smoked salmon trimmings**
- **290 g/10 oz can baby clams**
- **2 tbsp freshly chopped parsley**
- **freshly grated Parmesan cheese, to serve**

### To serve:

- **green salad**
- **crusty bread**

## TASTY TIP

A good-quality stock will make a huge difference to the finished flavour of this risotto. Rinse 900 g/2 lb fish bones and trimmings and put in a large saucepan with 1 carrot, 1 onion and 1 celery stalk, all peeled and roughly chopped, 1 bouquet garni, 4 peppercorns and 900 ml/1½ pints cold water. Slowly bring to the boil, then skim. Cover and simmer for 30 minutes. Strain the stock through a fine sieve, cool and chill in the refrigerator for up to 2 days. After chilling, boil vigorously before using.

# Cod with Fennel & Cardamom

Fennel and cardamom are used frequently in the Mediterranean for their distinctive flavours, respectively of aniseed and lemon.

Preheat the oven to 190°C/375°F/Gas Mark 5. Place the garlic in a small bowl with the lemon zest/rind, juice and olive oil and stir well.

Cover and leave to infuse for at least 30 minutes. Stir well before using.

Trim the fennel bulb, slice thinly and place in a bowl.

Place the cardamom pods in a pestle and mortar and pound lightly to crack the pods. Alternatively, place in a polythene/plastic bag and pound gently with a rolling pin. Add the crushed cardamom to the fennel slices.

Season the fish with salt and pepper. Place onto four separate 20.5 x 20.5 cm/8 x 8 inch squares of baking parchment.

Spoon the fennel mixture over the fish and drizzle with the infused oil. Then fold the baking parchment over to enclose the fish and form a pocket. Place the pockets on a baking sheet and bake in the preheated oven for 8–10 minutes, or until cooked. Serve immediately in the paper pockets.

## INGREDIENTS    Serves 4

- **1 garlic clove, peeled and crushed**
- **finely grated zest/rind of 1 lemon**
- **1 tsp lemon juice**
- **1 tbsp olive oil**
- **1 fennel bulb**
- **1 tbsp cardamom pods**
- **salt and freshly ground black pepper**
- **4 x 175 g/6 oz thick cod fillets**

## FOOD FACT

When buying fresh fish, look for fish that does not smell. Any fish that smell of ammonia should be avoided. The flesh should be plump and firm-looking. The eyes should be bright, not sunken. If in doubt, choose frozen fish. This is cleaned and packed almost as soon as it is caught. It is often fresher and contains more nutrients than its fresh counterparts.

# Paella

Originally from Valencia, paella became known as Spain's national dish, although the Spanish consider it still to be a regional dish.

Rinse the mussels under cold running water, scrubbing well to remove any grit and barnacles, then pull off the hairy 'beards'. Tap any open mussels sharply with a knife, and discard if they refuse to close. Heat the oil in a paella pan or large heavy-based frying pan and cook the chicken thighs for 10–15 minutes until golden. Remove and keep warm.

Fry the onion and garlic in the remaining oil in the pan for 2–3 minutes, then add the tomatoes, peppers, peas and paprika and cook for a further 3 minutes. Add the rice to the pan and return the chicken with the turmeric and half the stock. Bring to the boil and simmer, gradually adding more stock as it is absorbed. Cook for 20 minutes, or until most of the stock has been absorbed and the rice is almost tender.

Put the mussels in a large saucepan with 5 cm/2 inches boiling salted water. Cover and steam for 5 minutes. Discard any with shells that have not opened, then stir into the rice with the prawns/shrimp. Season to taste with salt and pepper. Heat through for 2–3 minutes until piping hot. Squeeze the juice from one of the limes over the paella. Cut the remaining lime and the lemon into wedges, arrange on top of the paella. Sprinkle with basil, garnish with prawns and serve.

## INGREDIENTS    Serves 6

- **450 g/1 lb live mussels**
- **4 tbsp olive oil**
- **6 medium-sized chicken thighs**
- **1 onion, peeled and finely chopped**
- **1 garlic clove, peeled and crushed**
- **225 g/8 oz/¾ cup tomatoes, skinned, deseeded and chopped**
- **1 red and 1 green pepper, deseeded and chopped**
- **125 g/4½ oz/⅔ cup frozen peas**
- **1 tsp paprika**
- **450 g/1 lb/2¼ cups Arborio/risotto rice**
- **½ tsp turmeric**
- **900 ml/1½ pints/scant 1 quart chicken stock, warmed**
- **175 g/6 oz/1 cup large peeled prawns/shrimp**
- **salt and freshly ground black pepper**
- **2 limes**
- **1 lemon**
- **1 tbsp freshly chopped basil**
- **whole cooked unpeeled prawns/shrimp, to garnish**

# Spanish Omelette with Smoked Cod

This recipe is extremely versatile; add vegetables of your choice, or like the Greeks, use leftover vegetables in the omelette.

Heat the oil in a large, nonstick, heavy-based frying pan, add the potatoes, onions and garlic and cook gently for 10–15 minutes until golden brown, then add the red pepper and cook for 3 minutes.

Meanwhile, place the fish in a shallow frying pan and cover with water. Season to taste with salt and pepper and poach gently for 10 minutes. Drain and flake the fish into a bowl, pour in the melted butter and cream, adjust the seasoning and reserve.

When the vegetables are cooked, drain off any excess oil and stir in the beaten eggs and parsley. Pour the fish mixture over the top and cook gently for 5 minutes, or until the eggs become firm.

Sprinkle the grated cheese over the top and place the pan under a preheated hot grill/broiler. Cook for 2–3 minutes until the cheese is golden and bubbling. Carefully slide the omelette onto a large plate and serve immediately with plenty of bread and salad.

## INGREDIENTS    Serves 3-4

- **3 tbsp sunflower oil**
- **3 potatoes, peeled and diced**
- **2 onions, peeled and cut into wedges**
- **2–4 large garlic cloves, peeled and thinly sliced**
- **1 large red pepper, deseeded, quartered and thinly sliced**
- **125 g/4½ oz smoked cod**
- **salt and freshly ground black pepper**
- **25 g/1 oz/¼ stick butter, melted**
- **1 tbsp double/heavy cream**
- **6 medium/large eggs, beaten**
- **2 tbsp freshly chopped flat-leaf/Italian parsley**
- **50 g/2 oz/½ cup grated mature Cheddar cheese**

**To serve:**
- **crusty bread**
- **tossed green salad**

## HELPFUL HINT

For best results, Spanish omelettes should be cooked slowly until set. Finishing the dish under the grill gives it a delicious golden look.

# Asia

The West Asian countries of Turkey, Syria, Lebanon and Israel all have Mediterranean coastlines; each with its own style of cuisine.

# Turkey

Although the Mediterranean regions of Turkey use fresh fruit, vegetables and fish, the other regions definitely have their own style of cuisine. Heavily influenced by the Ottoman Dynasty for six centuries, and by western countries in more recent years, Turkish cuisine has become world famous. The temperate climate and the country's long history of farming and cooking make it unsurprising that Turkish food has become a popular option in most European countries. Turkey is known for a diversity of dishes because of its rich flora, fauna and regional differentiation.

Like most Mediterranean countries Turkey still has some regional specialities. The north is famous for corn and anchovies, the southeast for dishes similar to those in Greece, like the sweet pastries baklava and kadayif, as well as kebabs, and central Anatolia shows an Italian influence in its love of pasta dishes. This diverse and traditional cuisine is an integral aspect of Turkish culture. It is a part of their rituals and of everyday life, reflecting spirituality through symbolism and practice.

Bread dough, or ekmek, is one Turkish speciality, which originated with the Ottomans, that forms the basis of many of their traditional meals. The dough is used to make many varieties of bread and also dumplings, one of which is Manti.

These dumplings are filled with meat mix and eaten with garlic yogurt, melted butter and paprika.

Kebabs are another favourite throughout the country, originating with the nomadic Turks, who grilled their meat over camp fires. Shish kebab is grilled cubes of skewered meat, whilst doner kebabs are made from stacked alternating layers of minced meat and sliced leg of lamb. These are rotated on a large upright skewer, in front of a vertical grill and, as they cook, thin slices are shaved and served.

Syria

The Syrian Arabic Republic lies on the eastern coast of the Mediterranean Sea, with Lebanon, Israel, Jordan, Iraq and Turkey as its border countries. With agriculture a primary industry for thousands of years, fresh produce has always been an important aspect of Syrian food. Despite numerous conquests from the Greeks, the Romans and the Persians, the Arabic culture has been maintained in Syria to a large extent, however many Syrian dishes have also been strongly influenced by the Greeks, the Asians, the Turkish and the French, mainly because of Syria's important position on the former east-west  Silk Road or trade route.

Syrian recipes include many dishes that use rice or flat bread, meat, vegetables, beans, sweets and fruits. The flat bread, or pitta, is served at most meals and is used for dipping into pastes and salads. Steamed bulgur wheat is added to meat in many Syrian dishes, most notably kibbeh, which is a minced lamb main course and is considered to be one of Syria's national dishes. Garlic is used frequently and olive oil and purified butter are the main fats used. Also popular are houmous (chickpea and tahini dip) and falafel (fried ground chickpeas), as well as makkadem, which is a dish made from sheep's feet. In the Mediterranean Sea region of Syria, spiced yogurt is a speciality.

Meze, or small sampler-type dishes, such as alangi (stuffed vine leaves) and shanklish, a tangy sheep's cheese, are eaten regularly, as is a dish called muhammara, a spicy dip of chopped walnuts and red pepper, which is frequently served with chicken kebabs. Syrians also have a reputation for cheese making, particularly a stringy cheese called jibbneh mashallale, and for enjoying particularly sweet or particularly sour foods; they have the highest sugar consumption rate in the world.

The Western Asian Lebanese Republic, which is the smallest country in the Middle East, lies on the eastern shore of the Mediterranean Sea. Home to various cultures through the centuries, particularly the Persians, Greeks, Romans, Arabs and Ottoman Turks, as well as the French in more recent times, Lebanon's cuisine has taken elements from each of these civilizations. Lebanon experiences mild, wet winters and hot, dry summers and the locals rear goats in the inland rugged mountainous regions of the country.

# Lebanon

The country's diverse culture is epitomized in its menus, from Greek and Turkish-type lamb dishes to the French influence on desserts, custards and croissants. Croissants stuffed with lamb, fish or chicken have evolved as a result of this French influence. Lebanese cuisine is also a mixture of the different specialities of each region and is considered to be a well-balanced, healthy diet, rich in fruit, vegetables, olive oil, herbs and spices. Muslims are forbidden to eat pork and it is not a popular meat with Lebanese Christians. Along the Mediterranean coast the

country's capital and main seaport, Beirut, is renowned for its spicy fish (samkeh harra) and octopus (akhtabout). Lebanon also has a long history of olive oil production, with the different regions producing different types of olive and therefore slightly different versions of oil.

Throughout Lebanon the main ingredient of any recipe is freshness. They use seasonal fruit and

vegetables rather than those grown in a greenhouse and the subtle use of herbs and spices, all of which are readily available in the souks (markets). One recipe that is well known in all regions of Lebanon is tabbouleh, made from parsley, mint, spring onions, tomatoes, bulgur wheat, lemon juice, olive oil and seasoning and served on a bed of lettuce.

Israel

Situated at the eastern edge of
the Mediterranean Sea, Israel
has deserts, mountain ranges
and coastal plains, meaning
temperatures vary enormously throughout the
country. Along the temperate Mediterranean coastline,
citrus fruit trees are grown, as are figs, pomegranates
and olives. With a diverse culture and religious
traditions, Jewish Israel has an equally diverse cuisine.
Many Israeli recipes were brought by Jews originating
in Asia and North Africa (Mizrahi Jews), whilst others
were brought to the country by those emigrating
from Eastern Europe and the western cultures and
are more typical of traditional Jewish food from
Hungary and Poland, as well as Russia.

Typical Israeli foods include flat bread, lentils, fresh fruits and nuts,
stuffed vegetables, grilled lamb and beef, dairy products – including
goat's cheese and many types of yogurt – and traditional spicy
Mediterranean salads and spreads, such as fava bean spread. Some
of the most typical dishes are stews, schnitzel (veal, chicken or
turkey cutlets), cheese-filled crepes (blintzes), matzo balls
(dumplings eaten with chicken soup) and latkes (potato pancakes).
Sweets, made from honey and sesame seeds, are also popular.

A small percentage of Israel's recipes are kosher, meaning meat
and milk products cannot be served during the same meal and
the consumption of certain types of animals is banned. Basically,

kosher meat must come from
animals that have cleft hooves and
chew their cud (so pork and other
products that come from pigs are
not to be eaten) and an animal must have been slaughtered
quickly and under supervision of religious authorities for the
meat to be considered kosher.

Main meals in Israel often start with a meze appetizer, which
could include dips and stuffed vegetables. The soup and main
course usually contains chicken or lamb, and fresh fruit or
Middle Eastern pastries, such as baklava, are served as dessert.

Mediterran

# Vegetables

**All the countries in the Mediterranean region boast the freshness of sun-kissed vegetables due to the temperate climate they enjoy and thus the perfect growing conditions experienced.**

All types of freshly picked vegetables are bursting with vitamins, they are cheap for the cook to use and recipes can often be amended to ensure that the cheapest, most seasonal ones are substituted through various times of the year. Vegetables are extremely versatile and can be used as starters, to accompany a main course of meat or fish, or for vegetarians and vegans dishes can easily be a tasty meal in themselves.

# Chunky Vegetable & Fennel Goulash with Dumplings

One of the less obvious elements of the diverse melting pot that is Mediterrean cuisine, Goulash is eaten in the South Slavic countries such as Slovenia (see page 84).

Cut the fennel bulbs in half widthways. Thickly slice the stalks and cut the bulbs into 8 wedges. Heat the oil in a large saucepan or flameproof casserole. Add the onion and fennel and cook gently for 10 minutes until soft. Stir in the paprika and flour.

Remove from the heat and gradually stir in the stock. Add the chopped tomatoes, potatoes and mushrooms. Season to taste with salt and pepper. Bring to the boil, reduce the heat and simmer for 20 minutes.

Meanwhile, make the dumplings. Heat the oil in a frying pan and gently cook the onion for 10 minutes until soft. Leave to cool for a few minutes.

In a bowl, beat the egg and milk together, then add the onion, parsley and breadcrumbs and season to taste. With damp hands form the breadcrumb mixture into 12 round dumplings each about the size of a walnut.

Arrange the dumplings on top of the goulash. Cover and cook for a further 15 minutes, until the dumplings are cooked and the vegetables are tender. Serve immediately.

## INGREDIENTS        Serves 4

- **2 fennel bulbs, weighing about 450 g/1 lb**
- **2 tbsp sunflower oil**
- **1 large onion, peeled and sliced**
- **1½ tbsp paprika**
- **1 tbsp plain/all-purpose flour**
- **300 ml/½ pint/1¼ cups vegetable stock**
- **400 g/14 oz can chopped tomatoes**
- **450 g/1 lb potatoes, peeled and cut into 2.5 cm/1 inch chunks**
- **125 g/4 oz/1¼ cups small button mushrooms**
- **salt and freshly ground black pepper**

### For the dumplings:
- **1 tbsp sunflower oil**
- **1 small onion, peeled and finely chopped**
- **1 medium/large egg**
- **3 tbsp milk**
- **3 tbsp freshly chopped parsley**
- **125 g/4 oz/2 cups fresh white breadcrumbs**

## TASTY TIP

Sour cream or crème fraîche would be delicious spooned on top of the goulash.

# Light Ratatouille

A classic Provençale dish, this is served hot or cold, as an accompaniment to meat or fish, or as the basis for a Mediterranean-style omelette.

Deseed the peppers, remove the membrane with a small sharp knife and cut into small dice. Thickly slice the courgettes and cut the aubergine into small dice. Slice the onion into rings.

Place the tomatoes in boiling water until their skins begin to peel away. Remove the skins, cut into quarters and remove the seeds.

Place all the vegetables, including the mushrooms, in a saucepan with the tomato juice and basil. Season to taste with salt and pepper. Bring to the boil, cover and simmer for 15 minutes, or until the vegetables are tender. Remove the vegetables with a slotted spoon and arrange in a serving dish.

Bring the liquid in the pan to the boil and boil for 20 seconds until it is slightly thickened. Season to taste with salt and pepper. Pass the sauce through a sieve to remove some of the seeds and pour over the vegetables. Serve the ratatouille hot or cold.

### INGREDIENTS        Serves 4

- **1 red pepper**
- **2 courgettes/zucchini, trimmed**
- **1 small aubergine/eggplant, trimmed**
- **1 onion, peeled**
- **2 ripe tomatoes**
- **50 g/2 oz/¾ cup button mushrooms, wiped and halved or quartered**
- **200 ml/7 fl oz/¾ cup tomato juice**
- **1 tbsp freshly chopped basil**
- **salt and freshly ground black pepper**

### TASTY TIP

This dish is also delicious as a jacket potato filling.

# Sicilian Baked Aubergine

The sunny climate of the Italian island of Sicily is perfect for growing these large and very healthy purple vegetables.

Preheat the oven to 200°C/400°F/Gas Mark 6. Place the aubergine/eggplant on an oiled baking sheet. Cover the tray with kitchen foil and bake in the preheated oven for 15–20 minutes until soft. Remove the aubergine from the oven and leave to cool.

Place the celery and tomatoes in a large bowl and cover with boiling water. Remove the tomatoes from the bowl when their skins begin to peel away. Remove the skins, then deseed and chop the flesh into small pieces. Remove the celery from the bowl of water, chop finely and reserve.

Pour the sunflower oil into a nonstick saucepan, add the chopped shallots and fry gently for 2–3 minutes until soft. Add the celery, tomatoes, tomato puree/paste and olives. Season to taste with salt and pepper. Simmer gently for 3–4 minutes.

Add the vinegar, sugar and cooled aubergine to the pan and heat gently for 2–3 minutes until all the ingredients are well blended. Remove from the heat and leave to cool, then garnish with the chopped basil and serve cold with salad leaves.

## INGREDIENTS     Serves 4

- **1 large aubergine/eggplant, trimmed and cubed**
- **2 celery stalks, trimmed**
- **4 large ripe tomatoes**
- **1 tsp sunflower oil**
- **2 shallots, peeled and finely chopped**
- **1½ tsp tomato puree/paste**
- **5 large green pitted olives**
- **5 large black pitted olives**
- **salt and freshly ground black pepper**
- **1 tbsp white wine vinegar**
- **2 tsp caster/superfine sugar**
- **1 tbsp freshly chopped basil, to garnish**
- **mixed salad leaves, to serve**

## FOOD FACT

It has been suggested that foods which are purple in colour, such as aubergines, have particularly powerful antioxidants, which help the body to protect itself from disease and strengthen the organs.

# Vegetarian Cassoulet

This French recipe bursts with the natural flavours of herbs that have been added to the dried beans and vegetables.

Preheat the oven to 180°C/350°F/Gas Mark 4, 10 minutes before required. Drain the beans, rinse under cold running water and put in a saucepan. Peel 1 of the onions and add to the beans with the bay leaf. Pour in the water.

Bring to a rapid boil and cook for 10 minutes, then turn down the heat, cover and simmer for 50 minutes, or until the beans are almost tender. Drain the beans, reserving the liquor, but discarding the onion and bay leaf.

Cook the potatoes in a saucepan of lightly salted boiling water for 6–7 minutes until almost tender when tested with the point of a knife. Drain and reserve.

Peel and chop the remaining onion. Heat the oil in a frying pan and cook the onion with the garlic and leeks for 10 minutes until softened. Stir in the tomatoes, sugar, thyme and parsley. Stir in the beans, with 300 ml/½ pint/1¼ cups of the reserved liquor and season to taste. Simmer, uncovered, for 5 minutes.

Layer the potato slices, courgettes/zucchini and ladlefuls of the bean mixture in a large flameproof casserole. To make the topping, mix together the breadcrumbs and cheese and sprinkle over the top.

Bake in the preheated oven for 40 minutes, or until the vegetables are cooked through and the topping is golden brown and crisp. Serve immediately.

## INGREDIENTS    Serves 4

- **225 g/8 oz/1 cup dried haricot/ navy beans, soaked overnight**
- **2 medium onions**
- **1 bay leaf**
- **1.4 litres/2½ pints/1½ quarts cold water**
- **550 g/1¼ lb large potatoes, peeled and cut into 1 cm/½ inch slices**
- **5 tsp olive oil**
- **1 large garlic clove, peeled and crushed**
- **2 leeks, trimmed and sliced**
- **200 g/7 oz can chopped tomatoes**
- **1 tsp muscovado/dark brown sugar**
- **1 tbsp freshly chopped thyme**
- **2 tbsp freshly chopped parsley**
- **salt and freshly ground black pepper**
- **3 courgettes/zucchini, trimmed and sliced**

### For the topping:
- **50 g/2 oz/1 cup fresh white breadcrumbs**
- **25 g/1 oz/¼ cup Cheddar cheese, finely grated**

# Pasta with Courgettes, Rosemary & Lemon

Rosemary is one of the classics of the Provençale herb palette, the others being thyme, bay laurel, parsley and basil – also popular of course in the rest of the Mediterranean.

Bring a large saucepan of salted water to the boil and add the pasta. Return to the boil and cook until *al dente*, or according to the packet instructions.

When the pasta is almost done, heat the oil in a large frying pan and add the garlic. Cook over a medium heat until the garlic just begins to brown. Be careful not to overcook the garlic at this stage or it will become bitter.

Add the courgettes/zucchini, rosemary, parsley and lemon zest and juice. Cook for 3–4 minutes until the courgettes are just tender. Add the olives to the frying pan and stir well. Season to taste with salt and pepper and remove from the heat.

Drain the pasta well. Add to the frying pan. Stir until thoroughly combined. Garnish with lemon and fresh rosemary. Serve immediately.

## INGREDIENTS     Serves 4

- **350 g/12 oz/4½ cups dried pasta shapes, such as rigatoni**
- **1½ tbsp good-quality extra virgin olive oil**
- **2 garlic cloves, peeled and finely chopped**
- **4 courgettes/zucchini, thinly sliced**
- **1 tbsp freshly chopped rosemary**
- **1 tbsp freshly chopped parsley**
- **zest/rind and juice of 2 lemons**
- **25 g/1 oz/¼ cup pitted black olives, roughly chopped**
- **25 g/1 oz/¼ cup pitted green olives, roughly chopped**
- **salt and freshly ground black pepper**

**To garnish:**
- **lemon slices**
- **fresh rosemary sprigs**

## TASTY TIP

Look out for patty pan squashes – small yellow or green squashes, shaped a little like flying saucers. They would make a good substitute for the courgettes in this recipe as they have a similar flavour. Cut them in half vertically and cook as above.

# Courgette & Tarragon Tortilla

This substantial traditional Spanish omelette is traditionally made from eggs, potatoes and onions. Here, courgettes and tarragon are added for extra flavour and colour.

Peel the potatoes and slice thinly. Dry the slices in a clean dishtowel to get them as dry as possible. Heat the oil in a large heavy-based pan, add the onion and cook for 3 minutes. Add the potatoes with a little salt and pepper, then stir the potatoes and onion lightly to coat in the oil.

Reduce the heat to the lowest possible setting, cover and cook gently for 5 minutes. Turn the potatoes and onion over and continue to cook for a further 5 minutes. Give the pan a shake every now and again to ensure that the potatoes do not stick to the base or burn. Add the courgette/zucchini, then cover and cook for a further 10 minutes.

Beat the eggs and tarragon together and season to taste with salt and pepper. Pour the egg mixture over the vegetables and return to the heat. Cook on a low heat for up to 20–25 minutes, or until there is no liquid egg left on the surface of the tortilla.

Turn the tortilla over by inverting it onto a saucepan lid or a flat plate, then sliding it back into the pan. Return the pan to the heat and cook for a final 3–5 minutes, or until the underside is golden brown. If preferred, place the tortilla under a preheated grill/broiler for 4 minutes, or until set and golden brown on top. Cut into small squares and serve hot or cold with tomato wedges.

### INGREDIENTS     Serves 6

- **5–6 potatoes**
- **3 tbsp olive oil**
- **1 onion, peeled and thinly sliced**
- **salt and freshly ground black pepper**
- **1 courgette/zucchini, trimmed and thinly sliced**
- **6 eggs**
- **2 tbsp freshly chopped tarragon**
- **tomato wedges, to serve**

### HELPFUL HINT

Use even-sized waxy potatoes, which will not break up during cooking – Maris Bard, Charlotte or Pentland Javelin are all good choices. A sprinkling of grated cheese before finally returning to the heat gives this dish a good golden colour.

# Spring Vegetable & Herb Risotto

Why not try serving this tasty vegetarian option with Parmesan crisps or baked goats' cheese and rocket salad?

Bring the vegetable stock to the boil in a large saucepan and add the asparagus, baby carrots, peas and beans. Bring the stock back to the boil and remove the vegetables at once using a slotted spoon. Rinse under cold running water. Drain again and reserve. Keep the stock hot.

Heat the oil in a large deep frying pan and add the onion. Cook over a medium heat for 4–5 minutes until starting to brown. Add the garlic and thyme and cook for a further few seconds. Add the rice and stir well for a minute until the rice is hot and coated in oil.

Add the white wine and stir constantly until the wine is almost completely absorbed by the rice. Begin adding the stock a ladleful at a time, stirring well and waiting until the last ladleful has been absorbed before stirring in the next. Add the vegetables after using about half of the stock. Continue until all the stock is used. This will take 20–25 minutes. The rice and vegetables should both be tender.

Remove the pan from the heat. Stir in the herbs, lemon zest and crème fraîche/sour cream. Season to taste with salt and pepper and serve immediately.

## INGREDIENTS    Serves 2-3

- **1 litre/1¾ pints/1 quart vegetable stock**
- **125 g/4½ oz/½ cup asparagus tips, trimmed**
- **125 g/4½ oz/1 cup baby carrots, scrubbed**
- **50 g/2 oz/½ cup peas, fresh or frozen**
- **50 g/2 oz/½ cup fine French/green beans, trimmed**
- **1 tbsp olive oil**
- **1 onion, peeled and finely chopped**
- **1 garlic clove, peeled and finely chopped**
- **2 tsp freshly chopped thyme**
- **225 g/8 oz/1 heaping cup Arborio/risotto rice**
- **150 ml/¼ pint/⅔ cup white wine**
- **1 tbsp each freshly chopped basil, chives and parsley**
- **zest/rind of ½ lemon**
- **3 tbsp crème fraîche/sour cream**
- **salt and freshly ground black pepper**

# Broad Bean & Artichoke Risotto

Broad beans and artichokes are a classic combination, as here in an Italian risotto, or in a Greek stew, popularly served during Lent.

Cook the beans in a saucepan of lightly salted boiling water for 4–5 minutes, or until just tender. Drain and plunge into cold water. Peel off the tough outer skins, if liked. Pat the artichokes dry on absorbent paper towels and cut each in half lengthways through the stem end. Cut each half into 3 wedges.

Heat the oil in a large saucepan and cook the artichokes for 4–5 minutes, turning occasionally, until they are lightly browned. Remove and reserve. Bring the wine and stock to the boil in a separate frying pan. Keep them barely simmering while making the risotto.

Melt the butter in a large frying pan, add the onion and cook for 5 minutes until beginning to soften. Add the rice and cook for 1 minute, stirring. Pour in a ladleful of the hot wine and stock, simmer gently, stirring frequently, until the stock is absorbed. Continue to add the stock in this way for 20–25 minutes until the rice is just tender; the risotto should look creamy and soft.

Add the broad/fava beans, artichokes and lemon zesdt/rind and juice. Gently mix in, cover and leave to warm through for 1–2 minutes. Stir in the Parmesan cheese and season to taste with salt and pepper. Serve sprinkled with extra Parmesan cheese.

## INGREDIENTS     Serves 4

- **275 g/10 oz frozen broad/ fava beans**
- **400 g/14 oz can artichoke hearts, drained**
- **1 tbsp sunflower oil**
- **150 ml/¼ pint/⅔ cup dry white wine**
- **900 ml/1½ pints/scant 1 quart vegetable stock**
- **25 g/1 oz/2 tbsp butter**
- **1 onion, peeled and finely chopped**
- **200 g/7 oz/1 cup Arborio/ risotto rice**
- **finely grated zest/rind and juice of 1 lemon**
- **50 g/2 oz/½ cup Parmesan cheese, grated**
- **salt and freshly ground black pepper**
- **freshly grated Parmesan cheese, to serve**

## HELPFUL HINT

If using fresh broad beans, buy about 700 g/1½ lb in their pods. Young fresh beans do not need to be skinned.

# Potato Gnocchi with Pesto Sauce

This very simple and straightforward Italian recipe is ideal for vegetarian guests. Why not add some fresh olives too?

Cook the potatoes in their skins in boiling water for 20 minutes, or until tender. Drain and peel. While still warm, push the potatoes through a fine sieve/strainer into a bowl. Stir in the butter, egg, 175 g/6 oz/1½ cups of the flour and the salt and pepper.

Sift the remaining flour onto a board or work surface and add the potato mixture. Gently knead in enough flour until a soft, slightly sticky dough is formed.

With floured hands, break off portions of the dough and roll into 2.5 cm/1 inch thick ropes. Cut into 2 cm/¾ inch lengths. Lightly press each piece against the inner prongs of a fork. Put on a tray covered with a floured dishtowel and chill in the refrigerator for about 30 minutes.

To make the pesto sauce, put the basil, garlic, pine nuts and oil in a processor and blend until smooth and creamy. Turn into a bowl and stir in the Parmesan cheese. Season to taste.

Cooking in several batches, drop the gnocchi into a saucepan of barely simmering salted water. Cook for 3–4 minutes, or until they float to the surface. Remove with a slotted spoon and keep warm in a covered oiled baking dish in a low oven.

Add the gnocchi to the pesto sauce and toss gently to coat. Serve immediately, scattered with the Parmesan cheese and accompanied by a rocket/arugula salad.

## INGREDIENTS          Serves 6

- **900 g/2 lb floury potatoes**
- **40 g/1½ oz/3 tbsp butter**
- **1 medium/large egg, beaten**
- **225 g/8 oz/2 cups plain/all-purpose flour**
- **1 tsp salt**
- **freshly ground black pepper**
- **25 g/1 oz/¼ cup shaved Parmesan cheese**
- **rocket/arugula salad, to serve**

### For the pesto sauce:

- **50 g/2 oz/2 packed cups fresh basil leaves**
- **1 large garlic clove, peeled**
- **2 tbsp pine nuts**
- **120 ml/4 fl oz/½ cup olive oil**
- **40 g/1½ oz/scant ½ cup grated Parmesan cheese**

## HELPFUL HINT

Use a vegetable peeler to pare the Parmesan cheese into decorative thin curls.

# Spanish Baked Tomatoes

Tomatoes are a key element of Spanish cuisine. You can even see people revel in tomato goo during the huge tomato fight – the Tomatina – in Buñol, Valencia, every year.

Preheat the oven to 180°C/350°F/Gas Mark 4. Place the rice in a saucepan, pour over the vegetable stock and bring to the boil. Simmer for 30 minutes, or until the rice is tender. Drain and turn into a mixing bowl.

Add 1 teaspoon sunflower oil to a small nonstick frying pan and gently fry the shallots, garlic, pepper, chilli and mushrooms for 2 minutes. Add to the rice with the chopped oregano. Season with plenty of salt and pepper.

Slice the top off each tomato. Cut and scoop out the flesh, removing the hard core. Pass the tomato flesh through a sieve/strainer and add 1 tablespoon of the juice to the rice mixture. Stir in the beaten egg and mix. Sprinkle a little sugar in the base of each tomato, then pile the rice mixture into the shells.

Place the tomatoes in a baking dish and pour a little cold water around them. Replace their lids and drizzle a few drops of sunflower oil over the tops.

Bake in the preheated oven for about 25 minutes. Garnish with the basil leaves and season with black pepper and serve immediately with crusty bread.

## INGREDIENTS          Serves 4

- **175 g/6 oz/1 cup wholegrain rice**
- **600 ml/1 pint/2½ cups vegetable stock**
- **2 tsp sunflower oil**
- **2 shallots, peeled and finely chopped**
- **1 garlic clove, peeled and crushed**
- **1 green pepper, deseeded and cut into small cubes**
- **1 red chilli, deseeded and finely chopped**
- **50 g/2 oz/½ cup button mushrooms, finely chopped**
- **1 tbsp freshly chopped oregano**
- **salt and freshly ground black pepper**
- **4 large ripe beef tomatoes**
- **1 large/extra large egg, beaten**
- **1 tsp caster/superfine sugar**
- **basil leaves, to garnish**
- **crusty bread, to serve**

## TASTY TIP

This dish is also delicious when made with meat. Add 125 g/4 oz minced beef to the frying pan. Dry-fry the meat on a high heat until cooked through and brown, before adding the rest of the ingredients.

# Chargrilled Vegetable & Goats' Cheese Pizza

With so many fresh vegetables and no fatty meats, perhaps this pizza would tempt even the health conscious to try a slice, despite the cheese…

Preheat the oven to 220°C/425°F/Gas Mark 7, 15 minutes before baking. Put a baking sheet in the oven to heat up. Cook the potato in lightly salted boiling water until tender. Peel and mash with the olive oil until smooth.

Sift the flour and salt into a bowl. Stir in the yeast. Add the mashed potato and 150 ml/¼ pint/⅔ cup warm water and mix to a soft dough. Knead for 5–6 minutes until smooth. Put the dough in a bowl, cover with clingfilm/plastic wrap and leave to rise in a warm place for 30 minutes.

To make the topping, arrange the aubergine/eggplant, courgettes/zucchini, pepper and onion, skin-side up, on a grill/broiler rack and brush with 4 tablespoons of the oil. Grill for 4–5 minutes. Turn the vegetables and brush with the remaining oil. Grill for 3–4 minutes. Cool, skin and slice the pepper. Put all of the vegetables in a bowl, add the halved new potatoes and toss gently together. Set aside.

Briefly re-knead the dough, then roll out to a 30.5–35.5 cm/ 12–14 in round, according to preferred thickness. Mix the tomatoes and oregano together and spread over the pizza base. Scatter over the mozzarella cheese. Put the pizza on the preheated baking sheet and bake for 8 minutes.

Arrange the vegetables and goats' cheese on top and bake for 8–10 minutes. Serve.

## INGREDIENTS          Serves 4

- **125 g/4 oz baking potato**
- **1 tbsp olive oil**
- **225 g/8 oz/1¾ cups strong white bread flour**
- **½ tsp salt**
- **1 tsp easy-blend/active dried yeast**

### For the topping:
- **1 medium aubergine/eggplant, thinly sliced**
- **2 small courgettes/zucchini, trimmed and sliced lengthways**
- **1 yellow pepper, quartered and deseeded**
- **1 red onion, peeled and sliced into very thin wedges**
- **5 tbsp olive oil**
- **175 g/6 oz/1½ cups cooked new potatoes, halved**
- **400 g/14 oz can chopped tomatoes, drained**
- **2 tsp freshly chopped oregano**
- **125 g/4 oz/⅓ cup mozzarella cheese, cut into small cubes**
- **125 g/4 oz/⅓ cup goats' cheese, crumbled**

# Spinach, Pine Nut & Mascarpone Pizza

Traditionally, mozzarella cheese is used for pizza topping, but this recipe incorporates another Italian cheese – mascarpone – which gives a creamy textured result to complement the delicate spinach and pine nut topping.

Preheat the oven to 220°C/425°F/Gas Mark 7. Sift the flour and salt into a bowl and stir in the yeast. Make a well in the centre and gradually add the water and oil to form a soft dough.

Knead the dough on a floured surface for about 5 minutes until smooth and elastic. Place in a lightly oiled bowl and cover with clingfilm/plastic wrap. Leave to rise in a warm place for 1 hour.

Knock the pizza dough with your fist a few times, shape and roll out thinly on a lightly floured board. Place on a lightly floured baking sheet and lift the edge to make a little rim. Place another baking sheet into the preheated oven to heat up.

Heat half the oil in a frying pan and gently fry the onion and garlic until soft and starting to change colour.

Squeeze out any excess water from the spinach and chop finely. Add to the onion and garlic with the remaining olive oil. Season to taste with salt and pepper.

Spread the passata/tomato puree on the pizza dough and top with the spinach mixture. Mix the mascarpone with the pine nuts and dot over the pizza.

Slide the pizza onto the hot baking sheet and bake for 15–20 minutes. Transfer to a large plate and serve immediately.

## INGREDIENTS    Serves 2-4

### For the basic pizza dough:
- **225 g/8 oz/2 cups strong white/bread flour**
- **½ tsp salt**
- **¼ tsp quick-acting dried yeast**
- **150 ml/¼ pint/⅔ cup warm water**
- **1 tbsp extra virgin olive oil**

### For the topping:
- **3 tbsp olive oil**
- **1 large red onion, peeled and chopped**
- **2 garlic cloves, peeled and finely sliced**
- **450 g/1 lb/3 cups frozen spinach, thawed and drained**
- **salt and freshly ground black pepper**
- **3 tbsp passata/tomato puree**
- **125 g/4 oz/½ cup mascarpone cheese**
- **1 tbsp toasted pine nuts**

# North Africa

The shores of, from east to west, Egypt, Libya, Tunisia, Algeria and Morocco are all lapped by Mediterranean waters and consequently boast cuisines that offer a tantalizing fusion of Mediterranean and African characteristics.

Egypt

**The Arab Republic of Egypt is probably most famous for its ancient civilizations and the architectural treasures they left behind, such as the well-known pyramids at Giza, outside Cairo, and the tombs in the Valley of the Kings. The history of Egypt's food also stems from ancient times. Because of an incredibly dry climate the Ancient Eyptians relied on the flooding of the River Nile to irrigate their crops, which included wheat to make bread and barley to make beer. The Nile also produced fish, which provided the bulk of the protein for these ancient people, as the terrain was too dry and hot to rear livestock. The Ancient Egyptians were also fond of onion and garlic, a trend that has continued to the present day.**

In addition to ancient traditions, foreign influence is evident in modern-day Egyptian dishes, particularly that of Turkey, making many recipes a mix of Mediterranean and Middle Eastern trends, such as the dessert baklava, which is drenched in honey, and Turkish coffee, which is drunk regularly. Influence also came from the Romans, the Arabs, the Ottoman Turks, the Syrians, the Lebanese and the Palestinians.

Egyptians enjoy houmous (chickpea and tahini dip) and aubergine dip, both eaten with pitta bread strips. Many of their dishes are simple, with naturally ripened fruits and vegetables mixed with fresh local spices, although not made too spicy or hot. Meat is eaten in moderation; it is cooked with vegetables and served with rice, salad or pasta. Weddings, festivals and ceremonies are a time for feasting on traditional Egyptian dishes, when popular meats like pigeon, chicken, mutton, camel and buffalo are eaten. As with most Mediterranean countries, food is about company and the Egyptians make meal times a definite family time. They eat fava beans regularly, honey is their traditional source of adding sweetness to dishes and most households make their own bread either from white flour or from wholemeal flour.

# Libya

Next along the coast from Egypt lies Libya. It seems that the Berbers, during the Neolithic period, were the first civilization to introduce farming and cattle rearing to ancient Libya. Subsequent occupations, particularly by the Phoenicians, the Greeks, the Persians, the Romans, the Vandals and the Byzantines have all left their mark on modern-day Libyan cuisine to a greater

or lesser extent. Occupied by the Italians at the outbreak of the Second World War, much of Libya is desert, which means it has very high temperatures and very low rainfall.

Unsurprisingly, Libyan cuisine is a mix of Italian, Arabic and Mediterranean influences, with pasta dishes being popular, as well as the North African favourite of couscous, which in

Libya is served with braised lamb, vegetables and dried fruit. Fruit is grown throughout Libya and in particular the country produces apricots, nectarines, grapes, peaches, melons and all types of citrus fruit. Libya tends to have national dishes, as opposed to regional ones, and, although they may be prepared in slightly different ways, the basic concept is the same across the country. For religious reasons pork is not commonly served in Libya, and as a Muslim country there are many religious and national traditions about the way in which food is served and eaten. Food is served on a large platter and placed in the centre of the table so that all those eating can help themselves from the edge of the plate. The food in the centre of the plate is not eaten, but is offered to Heaven. Drinks are not served with meals, but a communal glass is handed around the table after the meal. Drinkers are not allowed to breathe until the glass has been removed from their lips.

The Republic of Tunisia has a diverse climate, with much of its southern region made up of the Sahara Desert. The Phoenicians, Romans, Vandals, Byzantines, Arabs, Spanish and French have all occupied Tunisia over the centuries. Though predominantly inherited from the nomadic tribes that originated in Tunisia, this series of conquests has affected the country's culture and the way its food is prepared and eaten.

# Tunisia

Harissa, a hot, red pepper sauce, together with chilli peppers, garlic, olive oil, tomatoes and spices such as coriander and cumin play an important role in Tunisian cuisine. Compared to countries like Egypt and Libya, the Tunisians prefer their food spicy and hot. They eat a wide range of seafood and have many traditional lamb recipes.

The country has a long Mediterranean Sea coastline and many busy fishing ports, so the preparation of fish dishes varies enormously; grilled, baked, fried and coated in batter are all popular dishes. Most fish dishes are served with sliced lemon and a drizzle of olive oil, although squid, cuttlefish and octopus are often stuffed and served with Tunisia's national dish of couscous.

Tunisians cook their couscous in a type of steamer or double boiler, with the vegetables placed in the lower section and the grain in the top half. As the steam from the vegetables rises, so

the couscous, made from the grain of semolina rice and ground wheat flour, is cooked. Couscous can be served with a variety of vegetables or with meats. In Tunisia it is usually served with lamb stew or broth. One traditional way in which Tunisians prepare young lamb is called 'coucha'. Shoulder of lamb is rubbed with olive oil, salt, mint, cayenne pepper and turmeric. The dish is oven-baked slowly in a tightly covered earthenware pot.

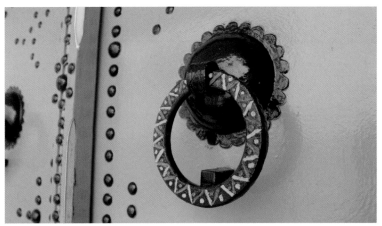

# Algeria

**The largest country on the Mediterranean Sea, the People's Republic of Algeria was formerly under Ottoman Turk rule but was invaded by the French in 1830 before it became independent in 1962. Most of Algeria's Mediterranean coastline is mountainous and the country's climate can range from extremely hot during the day to cool or chilly at night, with a high level of rainfall. Algeria's soil is very fertile and many locals are employed in the agriculture industry.**

Algerian cuisine can trace its roots to a number of ancient cultures that once ruled, visited or traded with the country. Berber tribesmen marked the beginning of wheat cultivation, smen (cooked butter) and consumption of fruit such as dates; the Carthaginians created couscous; the Romans grew grain; Muslim Arabs introduced saffron, nutmeg, ginger, cloves and cinnamon from the 'Spice Islands' of Eastern Indonesia; and the French brought their breads.

Algerians prefer lamb, chicken or fish to be placed on a bed of warm couscous, accompanied by cooked vegetables such as carrots, chickpeas or tomatoes and they also enjoy spicy stews. They use couscous in desserts by adding a variety of ingredients, such as cinnamon, nutmeg, dates and figs (fig trees grow in abundance in the Algeria's desert regions). Bread is eaten with most meals and is usually French bread or flat bread like pitta.

As an Islamic nation, Algeria celebrates Ramadan each year. During this time they are not allowed to eat or drink between the hours of sunrise and sunset. At the end of Ramadan there is a feast comprising soup as a starter and lamb or beef as the main dish, although families living close to the Mediterranean Sea often substitute the meat with a fresh fish dish. Fresh fruit is usually served as the dessert at these celebrations.

Morocco

**The Kingdom of Morocco gained its political independence from France in 1956. Bordered by the Strait of Gibraltar to the north and the Sahara Desert to the south, Morocco's coastal plains are rich and fertile and the climate is ideal for the agricultural industry.**

With a very diverse cuisine, the country's choice of dishes has been heavily influenced over the centuries by the many different civilizations that have occupied it, namely the Berbers, the Spanish, the Corsicans, the Portuguese, the Moors, the Turks, the Arabs and the Jews. Home-grown citrus fruits, spices such as saffron, herbs such as mint and coriander and a plentiful supply of home-grown olives are all put to good use in Moroccan dishes. The country breeds sheep, cattle and poultry

and uses the Mediterranean Sea as its plentiful source of fish. They use a number of spices to enhance the flavour of meat and fish dishes, including cinnamon, cumin, ginger, turmeric, paprika and sesame and anise seeds. Couscous is eaten regularly with vegetables, meat and fish and as a dessert.

Many Moroccan housewives make their own bread daily from semolina flour. It is prepared in the family's kitchen and marked before being sent to the bakery for cooking. Sweet Moroccan mint tea is usually taken with meals, although absinthe and pine nuts are added when mint is not plentiful. This is a green tea prepared for guests by the head of the family, although the way in which this ceremonial tea is prepared varies from one region to another. It is served in small glasses and skilfully poured from a height to give it a frothy head, returning the tea to the pot several times before serving it to the guest; this gives it a stronger flavour.

# Desserts

Despite the fact that most Mediterranean people are not great dessert eaters, what they do enjoy is eating locally grown fruits when they are in season, picked straight from the trees.

Because fruits like figs, as well as soft fruits such as raspberries and peaches, grow in abundance, they can all be incorporated into recipes to tempt the guest or diner. In the wintertime, when fresh fruits are not so readily available, many of these recipes could easily be amended to incorporate dried fruits from the store cupboard and delicious cheese, nut and fruit combinations, not to mention chocolate!

# Raspberry Soufflé

Soufflés seem to have originated in France by the end of the eighteenth century. Forget their reputation as difficult haute cuisine and have a go at creating this deliciously light fruity dessert.

Wrap a band of double thickness greaseproof/waxed paper around the outside of four ramekin dishes. Make sure that 5 cm/2 inches of the paper stays above the top of each dish. Secure the paper to the dish with an elastic band or sticky tape.

Place the redcurrants and 1 tablespoon of the sugar in a small saucepan. Cook for 5 minutes until softened. Remove from the heat, press through a sieve/strainer and reserve.

Place 3 tablespoons water in a small bowl and sprinkle over the gelatine. Allow to stand for 5 minutes until spongy. Place the bowl over a pan of simmering water and leave until dissolved. Remove and allow to cool.

Beat together the remaining sugar and the egg yolks until thick, pale and creamy, then fold in the yogurt with a metal spoon or rubber spatula until well blended.

Press the raspberries through a sieve and fold into the yogurt mixture with the gelatine. Whisk the egg whites until stiff and fold into the yogurt mixture. Pour into the prepared dishes and chill in the refrigerator for 2 hours until firm.

Remove the paper from the dishes and spread the redcurrant puree over the top of the soufflés. Decorate with mint sprigs and extra fruits and serve.

## INGREDIENTS　　Serves 4

- **125 g/4½ oz/1 cup redcurrants**
- **50 g/2 oz/¼ cup sugar**
- **1 sachet/3 tsp powdered gelatine**
- **3 medium/large eggs, separated**
- **300 g/½ pint/1¼ cup low-fat Greek/plain yogurt**
- **450 g/1 lb/4 cups raspberries, thawed if frozen**

### To decorate:
- **mint sprigs**
- **extra fruits**

## HELPFUL HINT

Soufflés rely on air, so it is important that the egg whites in this recipe are beaten until very stiff in order to support the other mixture.

# Crème Brûlée with Sugared Raspberries

Translating from the French as 'burnt cream', this delectable dessert has a very similar counterpart in Spain's crema Catalana.

Preheat the oven to 150°C/300°F/Gas Mark 2. Pour the cream into a bowl and place over a saucepan of gently simmering water. Heat gently but do not allow to boil.

Meanwhile, whisk together the egg yolks, 50 g/2 oz/¼ cup of the caster/superfine sugar and the vanilla essence. When the cream is warm, pour it over the egg mixture, whisking briskly until it is mixed completely.

Pour into 6 individual ramekin dishes and place in a roasting tin/pan.

Fill the tin with sufficient water to come halfway up the sides of the dishes.

Bake in the preheated oven for about 1 hour, or until the puddings are set. (To test if set, carefully insert a round bladed knife into the centre; if the knife comes out clean they are set.)

Remove the puddings from the roasting tin and allow to cool. Chill in the refrigerator, preferably overnight.

Sprinkle the sugar over the top of each dish and place the puddings under a preheated hot grill.

When the sugar has caramelized and turned deep brown, remove from the heat and cool. Chill the puddings in the refrigerator for 2–3 hours before serving.

Toss the raspberries in the remaining caster sugar and sprinkle over the top of each dish. Serve with a little extra cream if liked.

## INGREDIENTS          Serves 4

- **600 ml/1 pint/2½ cups fresh whipping cream**
- **4 medium/large egg yolks**
- **75 g/3 oz/⅓ cup caster/ superfine sugar**
- **½ tsp vanilla essence**
- **25 g/1 oz/2 tbsp demerara/light brown sugar**
- **175 g/6 oz/1½ cups fresh raspberries**

## HELPFUL HINT

Most chefs use blow torches to brown the sugar instead of placing the puddings under the grill, as this is the quickest way to caramelize the top of the dessert. Take great care if using a blow torch, especially when lighting. Otherwise use the grill, making sure that it is very hot and the dessert is thoroughly chilled before caramelizing the sugar topping. This will prevent the custard underneath from melting.

# Sweet-stewed Dried Fruits

Fruit drying has a long tradition in the Mediterranean, with the hot climates enabling quick, natural sun-drying. The long shelf-life of dried fruit meant that isolated island villages would always have nutritious foods when cut off by snow in winter.

Place the fruits, apple juice, clear honey and brandy in a small saucepan.

Using a small sharp knife or a zester, carefully remove the zest from the lemon and orange and place in the pan.

Squeeze the juice from the lemon and orange and add to the pan.

Bring the fruit mixture to the boil and simmer for about 1 minute. Remove the pan from the heat and allow the mixture to cool completely.

Transfer the mixture to a large bowl, cover with clingfilm/plastic wrap and chill in the refrigerator overnight to allow the flavours to blend.

Spoon the stewed fruit into 4 shallow dessert dishes. Decorate with a large spoonful of half-fat crème fraîche/sour cream and a few strips of the pared orange rind and serve.

## INGREDIENTS    Serves 4

- **500 g/1 lb 2 oz packet mixed dried fruit salad**
- **450 ml/¾ pint/1¾ cups apple juice**
- **2 tbsp clear honey**
- **2 tbsp brandy**
- **1 lemon**
- **1 orange**

### To decorate:
- **half-fat crème fraîche/sour cream**
- **fine strips pared orange rind**

## TASTY TIP

Why not plump for a Moroccan feel with this dish by choosing dried fruit with a selection of figs, apricots and prunes? Add 1 teaspoon whole cloves, a generous grating of fresh nutmeg and fresh root ginger and 2 cinnamon sticks to the fruit in step 1. Serve with the half-fat crème fraîche and sprinkle over a few chopped walnuts.

# Summer Fruit Semifreddo

This Italian dessert is bursting with goodness and will keep perfectly in the freezer as a standby for unexpected guests – but remember to allow to thaw to its semi-frozen state before serving.

Wash and remove stalks from the fruits, as necessary, then put them into a food processor or blender with the icing/ confectioners' sugar and lemon juice. Blend to a puree, pour into a jug and chill in the refrigerator until needed.

Remove the seeds from the vanilla pod by opening the pod and scraping with the back of a knife. Add the seeds to the sugar and whisk with the egg yolks until pale and thick.

In another bowl, whip the cream until soft peaks form. Do not overwhip. In a third bowl, whip the egg whites with the salt until stiff peaks form.

Using a large metal spoon (to avoid knocking any air from the mixture), fold together the fruit puree, egg yolk mixture, the cream and egg whites. Transfer the mixture to a round, shallow, lidded freezer box and put into the freezer until almost frozen. If the mixture freezes solid, thaw in the refrigerator until semi-frozen. Turn out the semi-frozen mixture, cut into wedges and serve decorated with a few fresh redcurrants. If the mixture thaws completely, eat immediately and do not re-freeze.

## INGREDIENTS  Serves 6-8

- **225 g/8 oz/2 cups raspberries**
- **125 g/4½ oz/1 cup blueberries**
- **125 g/4½ oz/1 cup redcurrants**
- **50 g/2 oz/½ cup icing/ confectioners' sugar**
- **juice of 1 lemon**
- **1 vanilla pod, split**
- **50 g/2 oz/¼ cup sugar**
- **4 large/extra-large eggs, separated**
- **600 ml/1 pint/2½ cups double/heavy cream**
- **pinch salt**
- **fresh redcurrants, to decorate**

# Baked Stuffed Amaretti Peaches

Eating al fresco? You could try heating this dessert in foil on the barbecue just before serving.

Preheat the oven to 180°C/350°F/Gas Mark 4. Halve the peaches and remove the stones. Take a very thin slice from the bottom of each peach half so that it will sit flat in a baking tray. Dip the peach halves in lemon juice and arrange in the baking tray.

Crush the Amaretti biscuits/cookies lightly and put into a large bowl. Add the almonds, pine nuts, sugar, lemon zest and butter. Work with the fingertips until the mixture resembles coarse breadcrumbs. Add the egg yolk and mix well until the mixture is just binding.

Divide the Amaretti and nut mixture between the peach halves, pressing down lightly. Bake in the preheated oven for 15 minutes, or until the peaches are tender and the filling is golden. Remove from the oven and drizzle with the honey.

Place two peach halves on each serving plate and spoon over a little crème fraîche/sour cream or Greek/plain yogurt, then serve.

## INGREDIENTS     Serves 4

- **4 ripe peaches**
- **grated zest/rind and juice of 1 lemon**
- **8 Amaretti biscuits/cookies**
- **50 g/2 oz/⅔ cup chopped blanched almonds, toasted**
- **50 g/2 oz/½ cup pine nuts, toasted**
- **3 tbsp light muscovado/golden brown sugar**
- **50 g/2 oz/½ stick butter**
- **1 medium/large egg yolk**
- **2 tsp clear honey**
- **crème fraîche/sour cream or Greek/plain yogurt, to serve**

# Goats' Cheese & Lemon Tart

This tasty, tangy tart tastes great served with crème fraîche or sour cream; it won't sit on the table untouched for long!

Preheat the oven to 200°C/400°F/Gas Mark 6, 15 minutes before cooking.

Rub the butter into the plain/all-purpose flour and salt until the mixture resembles breadcrumbs, then stir in the sugar. Beat the egg yolk with 2 tablespoons cold water and add to the mixture. Mix together until a dough is formed, then turn the dough out onto a lightly floured surface and knead until smooth. Chill in the refrigerator for 30 minutes.

Roll the dough out thinly on a lightly floured surface and use to line a 4 cm/1½ inch deep 23 cm/9 inch fluted flan tin/pan. Chill in the refrigerator for 10 minutes. Line the pastry case/pie crust with greaseproof/waxed paper and baking beans or kitchen foil and bake blind in the preheated oven for 10 minutes. Remove the paper and beans or kitchen foil. Return to the oven for a further 12–15 minutes until cooked. Leave to cool slightly, then reduce the oven temperature to 150°C/300°F/Gas Mark 2.

Beat the goats' cheese until smooth. Whisk in the eggs, sugar, lemon rind and juice. Add the cream and mix well. Carefully pour the cheese mixture into the pastry case/pie crust and return to the oven. Bake in the oven for 35–40 minutes, or until just set. If it begins to brown or swell, open the oven door for 2 minutes, then reduce the temperature to 120°C/250°F/Gas Mark ½ and leave the tart to cool in the oven. Chill in the refrigerator until cold. Decorate and serve with fresh raspberries.

## INGREDIENTS          Serves 4

- **125 g/4½ oz/1 stick butter, cut into small pieces**
- **225 g/8 oz/2 cups plain/all-purpose flour**
- **pinch salt**
- **50 g/2 oz/¼ cup sugar**
- **1 medium/large egg yolk**

### For the filling:
- **350 g/12 oz/1½ cups mild fresh goats' cheese**
- **3 eggs, beaten**
- **150 g/5 oz/¾ cup sugar**
- **grated zest/rind and juice of 3 lemons**
- **450 ml/¾ pint/1¾ cups double/heavy cream**
- **fresh raspberries, to decorate**

# Fig & Chocolate Bars

The fig adds a sunny Mediterranean feel and complements the chocolate in these deliciously chewy dessert bars, which can be frozen.

Preheat the oven to 180°C/350°F/Gas Mark 4, 10 minutes before baking. Lightly oil an 18 cm/7 inch square cake tin/pan. Place the butter and the flour in a large bowl and, using your fingertips, rub the butter into the flour until it resembles fine breadcrumbs.

Stir in the sugar, then, using your hand, bring the mixture together to form a smooth dough. Knead until smooth, then press the dough into the prepared tin. Lightly prick the base with a fork and bake in the preheated oven for 20–30 minutes, or until golden. Remove from the oven and leave the shortbread to cool in the tin until completely cold.

Meanwhile, place the dried figs, lemon juice, 125 ml/4 fl oz/½ cup water and the ground cinnamon in a saucepan and bring to the boil. Cover and simmer for 20 minutes, or until soft, stirring occasionally during cooking. Cool slightly, then puree in a food processor until smooth. Cool, then spread over the cooked shortbread.

Melt the chocolate in a heatproof bowl set over a saucepan of simmering water. Alternatively, melt the chocolate in the microwave, according to the manufacturer's instructions. Stir until smooth, then spread over the top of the fig filling. Leave to become firm, then cut into 12 bars and serve.

## INGREDIENTS      Makes 12

- **125 g/4 oz/1 stick butter**
- **150 g/5 oz/1¼ cups plain/ all-purpose flour**
- **50 g/2 oz/¼ cup soft light brown sugar**
- **225 g/8 oz/1½ cups ready-to-eat dried figs, halved**
- **juice of ½ a large lemon**
- **1 tsp ground cinnamon**
- **125 g/4 oz dark/bittersweet chocolate**

## HELPFUL HINT

If you are unable to find ready-to-eat figs, soak dried figs in boiling water for 20 minutes until plump. Drain well and use as above.

# Chocolate Crepes

If you want to vary this recipe, try serving the crepes with a raspberry sauce, or just nut-topped ice cream.

Preheat the oven to 200°C/400°F/Gas Mark 6, 15 minutes before cooking. To make the crepes, sift the flour, cocoa powder, sugar and nutmeg into a bowl and make a well in the centre. Beat the eggs and milk together, then gradually beat into the flour mixture to form a batter. Stir in 50 g/2 oz/¼ cup of the melted butter and leave to stand for 1 hour.

Heat an 18 cm/7 inch nonstick frying pan and brush with a little melted butter. Add about 3 tablespoons of the batter and swirl to cover the base of the pan. Cook over a medium heat for 1–2 minutes, flip over and cook for a further 40 seconds. Repeat with the remaining batter. Stack the crepes interleaving with greaseproof/waxed paper.

To make the sauce, place the mango, white wine and sugar in a saucepan and bring to the boil over a medium heat, then simmer for 2–3 minutes, stirring constantly. When the mixture has thickened, add the rum. Chill in the refrigerator.

For the filling, melt the chocolate and cream in a small heavy-based saucepan over a medium heat. Stir until smooth, then leave to cool. Beat the egg yolks with the caster/superfine sugar for 3–5 minutes, or until the mixture is pale and creamy, then beat in the chocolate mixture.

Beat the egg whites until stiff, then add a little to the chocolate mixture. Stir in the remainder. Spoon a little of the mixture onto a crepe. Fold in half, then fold in half again, forming a triangle. Repeat with the remaining crepes. Brush the crepes with a little melted butter. Bake in the pre-heated oven for 15–20 minutes, or until the filling is set. Serve hot or cold with the mango sauce.

## INGREDIENTS          Serves 6

**For the crepes:**
- **75 g/3 oz/⅔ cup plain/all-purpose flour**
- **1 tbsp unsweetened cocoa powder**
- **1 tsp caster/superfine sugar**
- **½ tsp freshly grated nutmeg**
- **2 eggs**
- **175 ml/6 fl oz/scant ¾ cup milk**
- **75 g/3 oz/⅔ stick unsalted butter, melted**

**For the mango sauce:**
- **1 ripe mango, peeled and diced**
- **50 ml/2 fl oz/¼ cup white wine**
- **2 tbsp golden caster/superfine sugar**
- **2 tbsp rum**

**For the filling:**
- **225 g/8 oz dark/bittersweet chocolate**
- **75 ml/3 fl oz/⅓ cup double/heavy cream**
- **3 medium/large eggs, separated**
- **2 tbsp golden caster/unrefined superfine sugar**

# Index

Dishes with fulll recipes are shown in *italic* type.

Mediterranean Cooking